Designed and produced by Albany Books
36 Park Street London W1Y 4DE

First published 1981
Published by Albany Books
Copyright © Albany Books 1981

House Editor: Hugo Kondratiuk
Art Direction: Elizabeth Cooke
Design: Malcolm White

ISBN 0 902935 20 8

Text photoset
by SX Composing Limited, Rayleigh, Essex

Printed and bound in Spain by Printer Industria Grafica SA.

DLB 3976 1981

Jacket photograph:
The 'City of George',
South African Railways
Class 24, 2-8-4.
(*Photo: Lou Johnson*)

Endpapers: Steam
locomotives wait to use a
turntable on the Deutsche
Bundesbahn (German
Federal Railways) (*M.
Mehltretter, ZEFA*)

Title page: A Pacific
locomotive pulls a passenger
train through the Scottish
Highlands in 1956. (*J. M.
Jarvis, ZEFA*)

Pages 8–9: This ALCO 2-8-0
was exported to Peru to run
the Cerro de Pasco Railroad,
the lowest mainline point of
which is 3700 metres (12 200
ft) above sea level. It is
pictured here on the line in
1930. (*Brian Fawcett*)

*Acknowledgement for illustrations
are due to the following:*
Hugh Ribbans *pages 26–27*;
Crown Copyright Science Museum
with additional artwork by
Hugh Ribbans *pages 186–7*.

Steam Trains
of the World

Steam Trains
of the World

Bill Hayes

Albany Books

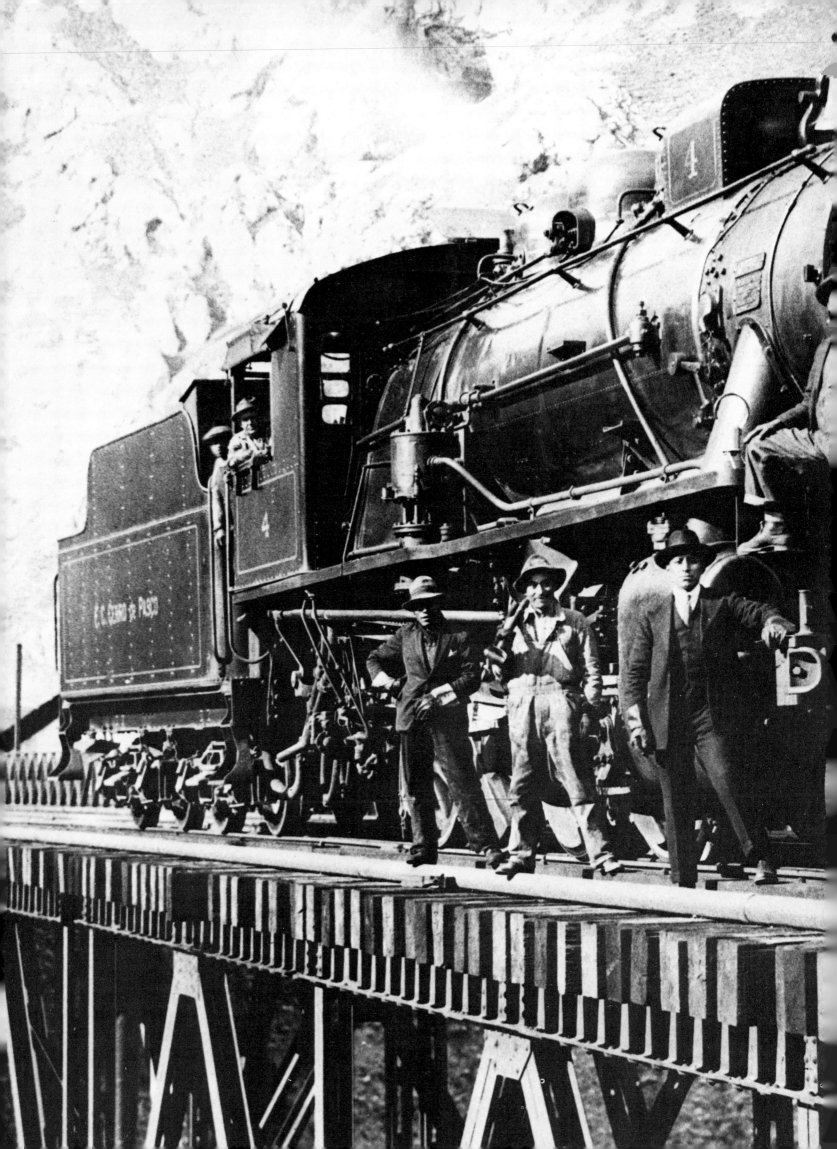

Contents

Introduction

The steam railway came about in the most humble of circumstances, almost by accident. Yet within a few decades it had swept irresistibly across the world, leaving hardly any aspect of life unaffected by the huge impact of its arrival. A product of industrialization, it stimulated in its turn the fast-growing new industries whose requirements had led to its birth. First in Britain, almost immediately in Europe and America, and eventually in every corner of the world, burgeoning railway networks acted as arteries, sustaining and extending the Industrial Revolution which changed for ever the pace and quality of life in the nineteenth century.

From its beginnings at a small colliery in England, the steam locomotive made its mark on most industrial countries within twenty years. Revolutionizing travel and communication, it hastened political and social changes in every country in which it appeared. It was for many people perhaps the first real fruit of the Industrial Revolution, the first concrete evidence that the new technology could be used to serve the general public as well as to impose upon it the hardships of factory labour.

In each country the story of railways has its own unique flavour. The country's terrain, the motives of the original speculators, and a host of conventional political considerations all combine to ensure that no two stories are alike. In this book we shall take a look at some of these stories, and examine just a few of the many thousands of steam locomotives that were built.

Like many readers, I missed, almost completely, the age of steam railways. With the exception of visits to preserved steam railways and terminals I have only two dim memories of steam trains. The first is of a day in 1953, when I watched the line being dismantled that ran along the end of my back garden in London. It took hours for the last train to creep off round the bend and out of sight. As the small tank engine with three or four wagons inched along, the men walking behind the procession ripped up the rails and slung them onto the trucks. Then they disappeared. It was a scene repeated in many parts of Britain, and in many other countries, at a time when railway systems were being severely cut down.

The second memory is of riding an express train to Fishguard, South Wales, on the Western Region. The blasts from its whistle echoed around the Welsh hills, as the train, puffing and rattling, hurled itself along. I remember sticking my head out of the window, and getting hot ash in my face for my pains. Not much to go on for a steam enthusiast in the way of first-hand experience. Yet somehow I found myself infected by the same excitement about these steam railways as people who might have travelled or worked on them for years. It is an infection

Top: Enthusiasts working on the restoration of an old steam engine, the *Drysllwyn Castle*, at Didcot, England. Countless locomotives have been restored in Britain, the U.S.A. and elsewhere through the dedication and hard work of train-lovers. (*Rick Cordell*)

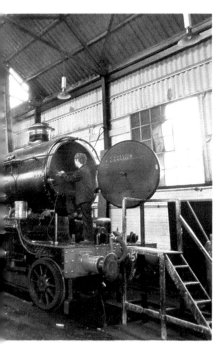

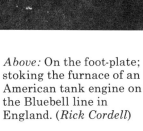

Above: On the foot-plate; stoking the furnace of an American tank engine on the Bluebell line in England. (*Rick Cordell*)

Above right: The stern notice adds an ironic touch to the final resting-place of this locomotive in the engine sheds at Didcot. (*Rick Cordell*)

shared by many thousands of people all over the world, especially in those countries where steam locomotives are either still running or have been lovingly preserved for the enjoyment of those too young to remember them in their working heyday. The sight of a steam engine in full cry, livery gleaming, pistons working frantically, steam belching from the chimney and trailing backwards like a streamer, today inspires in a new generation the same feelings of exhileration, awe and affection that characterized the appeal of railways for over a hundred years in the age of steam. This book will not explain those feelings, but I hope it may stimulate them.

Right: Horses had been used on 'tramways' long before the invention of the steam locomotive, particularly at collieries and iron works, and in some cases continued to be so until well into the steam age. This early photograph was taken at Denby colliery in Yorkshire. (*National Railway Museum*)

How it began

'If God had meant man to fly, He would never have given him the railways.' (Michael Flanders, *At the Drop of Another Hat*, 1964)

The great debate of the 1980s is, and will continue to be, about energy. With supplies of oil and other fossil fuels diminishing, the development of new energy sources, notably nuclear power, is being pushed forward with ever increasing urgency. This modern situation is fraught with its own complications, of course; yet in many ways it is almost a carbon copy, albeit on a much larger scale, of the circumstances surrounding the invention and subsequent use of the steam locomotive 150 years ago.

During the latter half of the sixteenth century wood, the most common source of energy until that time, was running out. The forests of England were being felled at an alarming rate. The coal **industry**, in its infancy at that time, was ill-prepared for the growing **demand** for greater yield. Most early mining had taken place on or near the surface in open cast mines. These seams were soon exhausted, forcing the mining industry to tackle the hazardous business of digging deep underground.

By 1690 the coal industry was in decline. Production had fallen, due to the enormous cost of sinking shafts and cutting galleries and the additional problems of flooding. The water which always collects in a mine was usually brought to the surface at that time by a series of buckets on a chain which were winched up by the power of a horse, and in some cases by hand. Plainly, this was a temporary solution. A new kind of horse power was needed – and that was hidden in the coal itself.

SURREY
Iron Railway.

The COMMITTEE of the SURREY IRON RAILWAY COMPANY,

HEREBY, GIVE NOTICE, That the BASON at *Wandsworth*, and the Railway therefrom up to *Croydon* and *Carſhalton*, is now open for the Uſe of the Public, on Payment of the following Tolls, *viz.*

For all Coals entering into or going out of their Bason at Wandsworth,	*per Chaldron,*	3d.
For all other Goods entering into or going out of their Bason at Wandsworth	*per Ton,*	3d.

For all GOODS carried on the said RAILWAY, as follows, viz.

For Dung,	*per Ton, per Mile,*	1d.
For Lime, and all Manures, (except Dung,) Lime-ſtone, Chalk, Clay, Breeze, Aſhes, Sand, Bricks, Stone, Flints, and Fuller's Earth,	*per Ton, per Mile,*	2d.
For Coals,	*per Chald. per Mile,*	3d.
And, For all other Goods,	*per Ton, per Mile,*	3d.

By ORDER of the COMMITTEE,

W. B. LUTTLY,
Clerk of the Company.

Wandsworth, June 1, 1804.

BROOKE, PRINTER, No. 35, PATERNOSTER-ROW, LONDON.

Left: At the beginning of the nineteenth century some horse-powered tramways were opened which could be used by anybody on payment of a toll, in much the same way as canals were operated. Here we see an advertisement for one such line running from Wandsworth to Carshalton, Surrey. (*Peter Newark's Historical Pictures*)

A Cornish plumber, Thomas Newcomen, designed and built the first atmospheric steam engine, later called the Cornish beam engine. When it was installed in a local mine in 1712, it soon became apparent that the problem of water in mines was well on the way to being solved. This engine dispensed with the buckets as well as the horse and pumped the water directly. Within a few years over 300 Newcomen engines were in use. Immediately coal production began to climb, from 3 million tonnes per annum in 1700 to 5 million in 1761 and to 10 million tonnes by the close of the century.

Other engineers started making variations of the new engine. James Watt made some fundamental changes, most important of which was his incorporation into the engine of the principle of reciprocating motion, using automatic valves. Watt was a very busy man and, contrary to the commonly accepted story, had little time to watch boiling

Right: Trevithick's *Catch-me-who-can* taking passengers on a circular pleasure trip in Euston Square, London, in 1808. (*Science Museum, London. Photo: Cooper-Bridgeman Library*)

Below: 'The Pitman', from George Walker's *The Costume of Yorkshire*, 1814. On the left is a steam locomotive built by Matthew Murray for John Blenkinsop, introduced in 1812 to haul coals from Middleton colliery near Leeds. (*The Mansell Collection*)

kettles on the hob. What he did see, however, was that if the up-down motion of the Newcomen engine could be adapted to rotate an axle, then the machine could in turn run looms, lathes and all manner of devices in factories. Within his lifetime Watt saw the landscapes of the Northern counties and Midlands of England become dotted with tall brick chimneys belching forth black smoke. His engines became the universal motors of the Industrial Revolution, while the economy, despite several short-term peaks and troughs, bulged with potential. The scene was set for the necessary and timely invention of the steam locomotive.

As the cotton mills, iron works and mines became increasingly dependent on coal, more and more attention was paid to improving the mining process. Thanks to Newcomen, the mines were dry and producing the required amount of coal, and getting it to the surface. However, a bottleneck was developing at the surface because the horses available could not pull the wagonloads of coal away quickly enough. For over 200 years the collieries had distributed their coal using horse-drawn carts that ran along crude wooden rails. With the outbreak of the Napoleonic wars, however, the price of horses and their feed rocketed, and soon they were in short supply.

At the turn of the century, Richard Trevithick had modified Watt's design so that it was almost portable. When in 1803 he was asked to build an engine to run a rolling mill, he made the daring suggestion that he might mount it on wheels and use it to replace the horse-drawn cart that brought the coal from the local mine. The owners of the mine agreed to this for an experimental period, and the first locomotive in the world went into service at the Penydarren colliery in Wales.

In the event, the *Trevithick I* cost more to run than a horse, and was consequently redirected to its original task. The point had been made however that steam traction was a practical alternative to the workhorse. Trevithick made more locomotives. One followed the *Trevithick I* into service at the Penydarren colliery, and another, the *Catch-me-who-can*, was put on public display at Euston, London. The owner of the Middleton colliery in Yorkshire saw this locomotive when he was in London. He was so impressed that he instructed his foreman of mines, John Blenkinsop, to organise the building of a locomotive to run along the tramline carrying coal into the centre of Leeds.

Blenkinsop commissioned the Mathew Murray Ironworks to construct the locomotive. The trouble with Trevithick's design was that the rails could not take the weight of engine needed for it to grip the track while doing the work required of it at the Middleton colliery. Therefore, Blenkinsop decided to lay a third rail along the track, with grooves cut into it into which a cog would mesh. The Blenkinsop engine was then able to haul itself along. It became known as the 'rack engine'.

One feature of the rack engine was to have two cylinders, so that when one was at the end of its stroke (dead centre of the drive wheel or cog) the other was only half way through. This ensured continuous motion. There was to be no more pushing of steam locomotives. In 1812, while Moscow burned, the first Blenkinsop engine was being tested at the Middleton colliery. The engine was called the *Prince Royal*, and was a great success.

Straight away the colliery ordered three more: the *Salamanca*, the

Left: A contemporary print of one of George Stephenson's Killingworth locomotives, dated about 1815–20. (*Photo: Science Museum, London*)

Far left: William Hedley discarded Blenkinsop's 'rack' and presented his *Puffing Billy,* so called because of the noise made by the exhausted steam. (*Photo: Science Museum, London*)

Below: The Hetton colliery, where many early engines built by George Stephenson were put to work. (*Photo: Science Museum, London*)

Right: George Stephenson's *Locomotion No. 1,* the first engine to ride the Stockton and Darlington Railway. Since 1857 it has been on display outside North Road station in Darlington. (*British Rail photo/MARS*)

Lord Wellington and the *Marquis Wellington.* Later, one of these engines was put to work in Wylam colliery in Northumberland, where the chief engineer, William Hedley, had ideas of his own on improving the rack engine still further. Eventually Hedley became a notable locomotive builder in his own right. His first, and most famous, engine, the *Puffing Billy,* was unwrapped in 1813. Whereas Blenkinsop was convinced that steam locos would have insufficient grip on the track without a third rail, Hedley successfully discarded the rack idea, proving his belief in the adhesion of his *Puffing Billy.* It did the work of ten horses transporting coal at Wylam. Hedley followed it up with two more engines for the colliery, the *Wylam Dilly* and *Lady Mary.*

Meanwhile, George Stephenson, chief engineer at the nearby Killingworth colliery, had been taking a keen interest in steam locomotives, eventually building his own, called the *Blucher.* This engine worked as well as, but no better than, the three Hedley engines or Blenkinsop's 'rack'. Stephenson agreed with the direction that Hedley's design had taken, but decided to tackle the problem from an entirely different angle, and sought to redesign the rails themselves. In 1816, he patented a wrought iron rail with a smoothly rounded head and overlapping joints. Previously the rails had been made of very uneven cast iron, butted flat and laid end to end, and this new design of Stephenson's allowed for much better wheel-to-track adhesion. This rail design has been universally adopted ever since.

Stephenson then returned to locomotive design itself, and set about suspending the works of the engine, thus protecting them as much as possible from vibration and allowing the axles a certain amount of movement up and down. On his second Killingworth engine, Stephenson fitted leaf springs, but they were very crude due to the poor quality of the iron available. The third engine had cylinders fitted vertically beneath the boiler, with the downward projecting piston rods latched onto the axle boxes. The steam pressure in the boiler floated the barrel of the engine above the axles, thus losing much of the vibration. This arrangement was not unlike the shock absorbers found in modern motor cars. As steel production improved, this steam suspension system was replaced with much stronger leaf springs. Stephenson built one

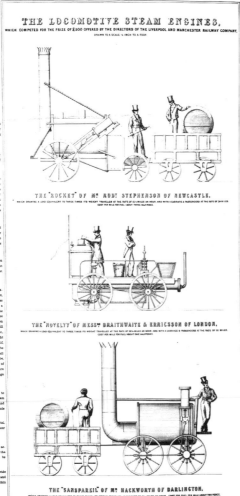

Left: The event which
finally established the
railway train was the
Rainhill trials of 1829,
organized by the owners of
the Liverpool and
Manchester Railway
Company. (*Photo: Science
Museum, London*)

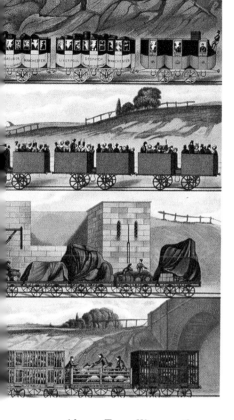

Above: Travelling on the Liverpool and Manchester Railway in 1831, showing the contrasting types and classes of rail travel which were established at the very beginning of public railways. (*Peter Newark's Historical Pictures*)

Left: A train crossing the Chat Moss bog near Manchester on the Liverpool and Manchester Railway, built by George Stephenson. (*The Mansell Collection*)

more engine in this series, which went into service with the others at the Killingworth colliery.

Stephenson's early engines, like Hedley's, had a chain drive device that distributed the power to the drive wheels. When he was asked to build an engine for the Hetton colliery, Stephenson replaced the chain drive with connecting rods leading straight from the piston rods. This innovation was a feature of steam locomotives right up to the last engine to be built. The Hetton locomotive itself stayed in service until 1908. Having completed it, Stephenson made a decisive move that turned a new page in the history of steam locomotion. With the help of his son, Robert, he opened the world's first steam locomotive workshop on the outskirts of Newcastle in 1823.

Meanwhile, in county Durham, more deposits of coal were found. Edward Pease, a rich mill owner, submitted a tender to build a railway or tramway line between Stockton and Darlington. After seeing the engines at Killingworth, Pease gave Stephenson the job of chief engineer for the new line. At Stephenson's request Timothy Hackworth, a young engineer later to design many steam engines of his own, was also employed.

The Stockton and Darlington Railway was opened in 1825, using a Stephenson engine called *Locomotion*. The first train set off down the line to loud applause at a tentative 5 km/h (3 mph). The public had not had a chance to see these new steam locomotives running before. The crowds marvelled and cheered as *Locomotion* crept along the line pulling a 70-tonne train. The engine could go faster, but so many spectators crowded the line that progress was slow. The *Locomotion*'s honeymoon period was soon over however; a month later, it blew up. Stephenson rebuilt it and it stayed on in service until 1841, when it was dismantled and put to work as a colliery pump. Eventually it was reassembled as a locomotive and set to rest outside North Road station, Darlington, where it has remained to this day.

In the year following the inception of the Stockton and Darlington line, some Manchester businessmen won a legal battle to build a line between Manchester and Liverpool. Who better to build it, they thought, than George Stephenson? He supervised the difficult job between 1826 and 1829. When the line was completed a choice of engine had still not been made and so a competition was held to find a suitable candidate to haul the first train. This much celebrated competition was known as the Rainhill trials.

Four engines entered, although only three arrived, the *Perseverance* having been damaged in transit. The three remaining engines arrived untested, virtually with their paint still wet. Two of the engines were the *Sans Pareil*, built by Hackworth, and the *Novelty*, a weird construction living up to its name, looking not unlike an early fire engine. The crowds fell in love with *Novelty* proclaiming it to be a 'gentleman's engine'. The last entrant was the *Rocket* built by Stephenson himself. As all the world knows, *Rocket* was the winner, taking the prize of £500, thus incurring a loss of £50 since it had cost £550 to construct. The *Rocket* ran a series of tests over 97 kilometres (60 miles), averaging a speed of 39 km/h (24 mph).

Alas, both *Novelty* and *Sans Pareil* developed trouble and were disqualified by default from the contest. Hackworth never got over the blow of this misfortune, and he blamed Stephenson for the crack that

appeared in one of his cylinders. Stephenson had cast the cylinder cases for Hackworth in his Newcastle shop. Hackworth suspected sabotage. The Manchester and Liverpool railway bought the *Sans Pareil* for £500 and ran it until 1844 but this did not heal Hackworth's wounded pride.

In true competitive spirit the *Rocket* had been designed to win the £500, but it had been conceived and built so well that the prototype was put into service for more than a decade on the M & L, hauling both passengers and freight. Eventually *Rocket* was demoted to pulling coal at the Earl of Carlisle's colliery at Brampton. The locomotive was withdrawn in 1840 and was finally wheeled into the Science Museum in London, where it is still exhibited.

The Rainhill trials are now world famous, but at the time they attracted only a limited amount of publicity. A year later the Manchester and Liverpool line was ready to be opened. The event received enormous amounts of publicity, set against a background of general industrial and social unrest amongst the working population. It was hoped by local businessmen that the opening of the line would act as a diversion, drawing the people's attention towards the technological revolution. The publicity campaign drew 400 000 people to the tracks, although the event itself did little to quell the social changes that were abroad in Britain; in fact the process of change hastened with each new mile of track laid.

Eight more *Rocket* type engines had been built for the line, and they all took part in the opening parade from Liverpool to Manchester. The *Northumbrian*, with George Stephenson on the regulator, pulled the special coach for the Duke of Wellington and the directors of the L & M company. Behind them came the *Phoenix, Rocket, Dart, Comet, Arrow, Meteor* and *North Star*. At 10.40 am the cortège moved off, travelling slowly so that ". . the spectators could enjoy their novelty, beauty and

splendour". Once outside Liverpool the procession speeded up. About 32 kilometres (20 miles) along the track, the trains stopped to refill with water and fuel. Then disaster struck! One of the guests in the coach carrying the Duke of Wellington was William Huskisson, an MP and economist. Climbing down from the coach to stretch his legs, he was struck down by the *Rocket* as it passed in the opposite direction. Huskisson was warned to get out of the way, but the door to the coach hung out over the other line, and he was trapped.

The *Northumbrian* was used to rush Huskisson to hospital, where he died that night. As he was being loaded aboard the train he remarked "I have met my death." The Duke of Wellington, like most present, was upset by the incident and wanted to cancel the proceedings and return to Liverpool. He was persuaded to continue because the Manchester crowds were reportedly getting very restless and so they carried on. The rain began to fall, and by the end of the day, with the trains returning to Liverpool in the dark six hours late, the future for railways in Britain, having suffered their first fatality, looked gloomy indeed. The despondency did not last long. Stanley, the famous explorer who presumed on Dr Livingstone, was one of the honoured guests on the first train, and wrote later: ". . . the adaptation of locomotive power was establishing a fresh era in the state of society, the final result of which it is impossible to contemplate."

George Stephenson continued to modify the *Rocket* engine design. He increased the size of the boiler, and lowered the cylinders to a horizontal position which reduced vibration and ensured steady running. By 1832 however, this design had outgrown its usefulness and Stephenson began working on his next family of locomotives, the 'Planet' class. This was followed by the 'Patentee' class, with six wheels arranged according to the formula 2-2-2.

This numbering system for wheel arrangements, which is still used

Above: This is the oldest working steam locomotive in the world, the *Lion*, built in 1838 for the Liverpool and Manchester Railway. The engine became famous when it appeared in the title role in the film *The Titchfield Thunderbolt.* (*John Adams/Colourviews*)

today to afford a quick and easy way of identifying a type of engine, was devised by a man named Whyte. The first digit denotes the forward free-running wheels, the middle number indicates the number of driving wheels, and the last digit represents the rear free-running wheels. All locomotives prior to the Patentee class were four-wheeled, all the wheels being drivers, so they were designated 0-4-0. The Patentee engine had free-running wheels front and back to support the longer boiler, and two driving wheels, hence, 2-2-2. It also had a shorter smoke stack, an inspection platform that ran around the perimeter, and the beginnings of a driver's cab. This engine became the direct ancestor of the modern steam locomotive.

The days of the four-wheeled locomotive were numbered, except in the mind of Edward Bury, an engineer who secured the franchise for transporting goods and passengers from London to Birmingham in 1836. He built a number of four-wheeled engines with the wheel arrangement 2-2-0. They were not very successful, often needing four engines to pull one freight train. He then fell in line with Stephenson and Hackworth and began building six-wheelers. The London and Birmingham line lost money and was eventually sold, leaving Bury out in the cold. Yet his engines were still in use, and soon other railways adopted some of his ideas in new constructions. The first locomotive to be built in Germany, the *Saxonia*, was copied from Bury's *Old Copper-knob*, so called because of the nipple atop the boiler.

The story so far has explained only the events that took place in

Above: A scene on the North Midland line, from a lithograph of 1840. The scene neatly contrasts the established, slow methods of transport – horse and canal barge – with the revolutionary speed of the steam train. (*Museum of British Transport. Photo: Cooper-Bridgeman Library*)

Above right: Detail of the second version of *First Class*, by Abraham Solomon (1824–62). The painting, from the mid-1850s, illustrates the elegance and comfort which already characterized railway travel for the rich. (*Roy Miles Fine Paintings. Photo: Cooper-Bridgeman Library*)

Right: Seats for Five Persons; in contrast to first class travel, the third class, as shown here by an unknown artist, could be far from comfortable in the early days of railways! (*National Railway Museum. Photo: Cooper-Bridgeman Library*)

Britain but at the same time similar advances were being made in railway construction in Europe and North America. Europe's first railway opened in France between Pont-de-l'Ane and Andrézieux in the St Etienne area, using an engine supplied by the Stephenson works. This railway was followed in 1830 by the opening of the first section of the St Etienne to Lyons line, eventually completed in 1832; and in the following years the rails spread through the rest of Europe. Many British locomotives were exported to America to supply the needs of pioneering railways there too.

More and more lines opened up in Britain. Eventually the bigger companies swallowed up or merged with the smaller ones until there were only a handful of regional companies left. During this initial period of rapid growth in railway travel the demands on locomotive engineers increased enormously, and it was a continual struggle for them to keep abreast of developments in design and technology. With each new engine that was rolled out of the locomotive shops another step was taken towards the ultimate exponents of steam like the *Mallard* and the massive North American 'Big Boys' of the 1930s. From the *Locomotion* which weighed only 3 tonnes, steam locomotives grew longer and faster for 100 years, culminating in the construction of the 'Big Boys' that weighed 350 tonnes and were 30 metres (97 feet) long, excluding the tender.

The designers of steam engines were forever setting new engineering standards. There was no problem that could not be solved; nothing, whether mountains or bog land, rivers or ravines, stood in the way of the railways as they spread across every country in the world. The steam locomotive has hauled countless millions of people, over an equally staggering number of miles, in their pursuit of work, war and holidays. Indeed, the notion of going to the seaside would not have been possible in the last century without the trains. Samuel Smiles wrote in his biography of Robert Stephenson, ". . . the locomotive gave a new celerity to time. It virtually reduced England to one sixth its size. It brought the country nearer to the town and the town nearer to the country. . . It energised punctuality, discipline, and attention and proved a moral teacher by the influence of example." With the opening of the Liverpool and Manchester railway the days of stage coaches and road tolls began to die. All previously established rhythms of travel and communication had been overturned by the ability of a steam train weighing 100 tonnes to move faster than any horse, virtually nonstop, between two centres of population.

Just as in today's arguments over road versus rail travel, there were many pressure groups who wanted to arrest the progress of the railways. Among these were the operators of canals and stage coaches, horse-sellers and those who simply feared that the entire output of coal and iron industries would be consumed by the advance of the steam engine. Many of these people were landowners, and they soon desisted when substantial compensation was offered to them in return for land used by the railways. So substantial was the compensation, that when British Railways was formed in 1949, it inherited the highest level of non-productive overheads of any railway system in the world.

Meanwhile the horse, against whose speed and strength the locomotive power of the steam engine was measured, retired to a long and well earned graze.

Right: A view of the high-level bridge at Newcastle-upon-Tyne, from a nineteenth-century engraving. The Industrial Revolution and its products, of which the railway was one, had a dramatic effect on the character and landscape of England's towns and cities. (*The Mansell Collection*)

New engines, new horizons

Now that we have seen the birth of the steam engine and the early development of railways, let us pause a moment to examine how a steam engine works, and how quickly it evolved into the type from which all successful locomotive designs followed, the 'long boiler' engine.

When water is heated to boiling point it begins to evaporate in the form of steam, and in so doing, it expands to 1600 times its original volume. Therefore, if the steam is restricted in some way, pressure builds up. This pressure, once applied, is a source of great mechanical energy or 'workpower'.

The action of a steam engine derives from the heating of a tank of

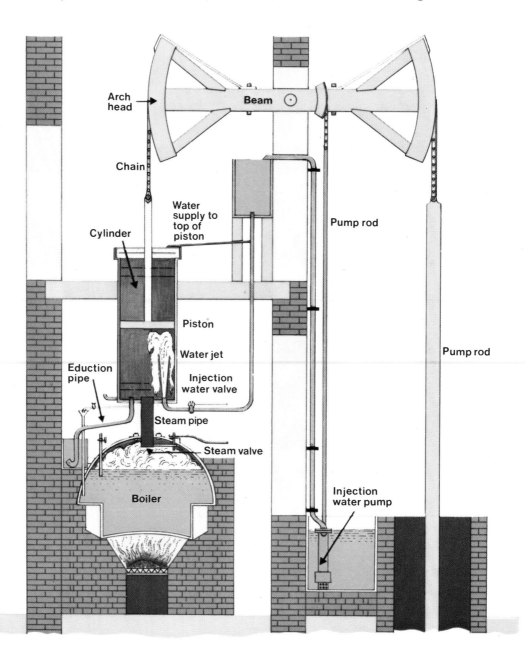

Right: Fig. 1. Thomas Newcomen's engine for pumping water, extensively used in collieries for over 70 years.

water (the boiler). The steam resulting from this is fed through a pipe from the top of the boiler to a cylinder, within which a piston is snugly fitted. The steam entering at one end pushes the piston down the cylinder. The piston is joined to a rod (the piston rod), which translates the movement of the piston into work.

The atmospheric engine

The original Newcomen engine was as clever as it was simple. As you can see from Fig. 1, the cylinder of this engine is vertical, with the piston rod rising and thus tilting a centrally pivoted beam, which in turn pushes downwards on a longer rod that operates a force pump. The pump was rather like the old stand pumps once found on English village greens.

When the steam has entered the cylinder, pushing the piston fully along, a jet of cold water is allowed into the cylinder which immediately cools the steam, condensing it back to its original volume. This creates a vacuum inside the cylinder. The air pressure on the piston forces it to sink to the bottom pushing out the cooling water from the cylinder. This pulls the beam down and pumps up water.

Below: Fig. 2. James Watt's double acting rotary engine, with the 'sun-and-planet' gear arrangement which enabled it to be applied to rotative motion and thus power the machines of the Industrial Revolution.

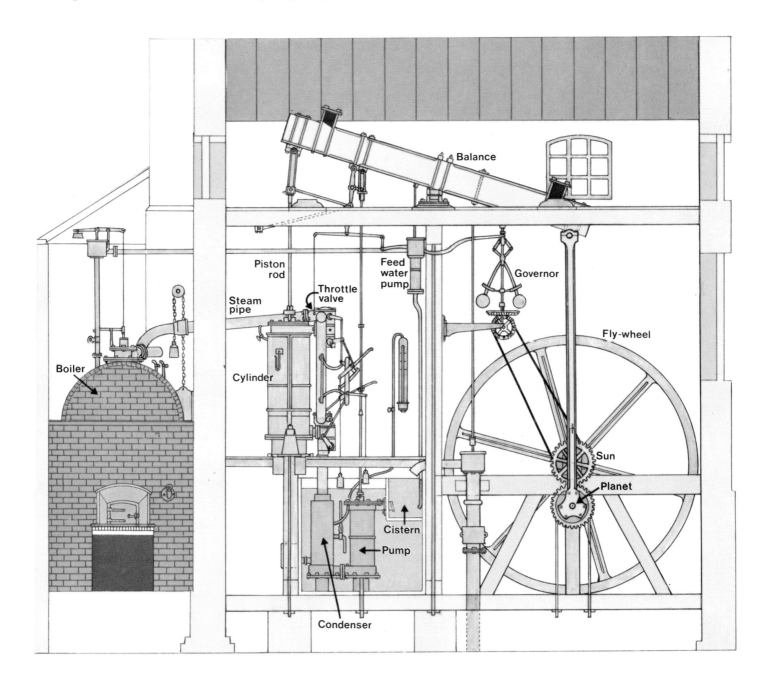

Balance

Piston rod

Feed water pump

Governor

Throttle valve

Steam pipe

Fly-wheel

Boiler

Cylinder

Sun

Planet

Cistern

Pump

Condenser

Unfortunately, this process was very crude, and required an operator to open and close the various valves during each cycle. Then one day, an operator by the name of Humphrey Potter connected a series of ropes and pulleys to the valves so they would work unattended, making the engine semi-automatic. This system was immediately refined and adopted. The Newcomen engine held its own in collieries for over 70 years. The device, with its great beam that rose and fell with a hiss and a puff, later became known as the Cornish beam engine.

James Watt's reciprocal motion engine

While repairing a Newcomen engine, James Watt saw that its basic flaw was that its method of cooling the cylinder involved a great waste of steam and heat. He was sure that to improve performance it was necessary to keep the cylinder jacket as hot as the incoming steam.

Watt began his improvements by introducing a small tank outside the cylinder. This tank, called the condenser, received and cooled steam and residual water pumped out of the cylinder by the motion of the piston. The next innovation was to close off the open end of the cylinder apart from a tight hole through which the piston rod could travel to and fro. Further, instead of allowing the atmospheric pressure to return the piston to the bottom of the cylinder in its own time, Watt introduced a secondary source of steam at the opposite end. This meant an equal pressure was acting upon both sides of the piston, thus giving the device a more continuous and reliable motion.

Watt then set about applying the much improved engine's capabilities to rotative motion. He had designed a crankshaft for this purpose, but unfortunately this method had just been patented by a man named Pickard, an acquaintance of Watt's. Instead of working with a man whom he considered a plagiarist of his ideas, Watt carried out his

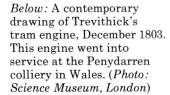

Below: A contemporary drawing of Trevithick's tram engine, December 1803. This engine went into service at the Penydarren colliery in Wales. (*Photo: Science Museum, London*)

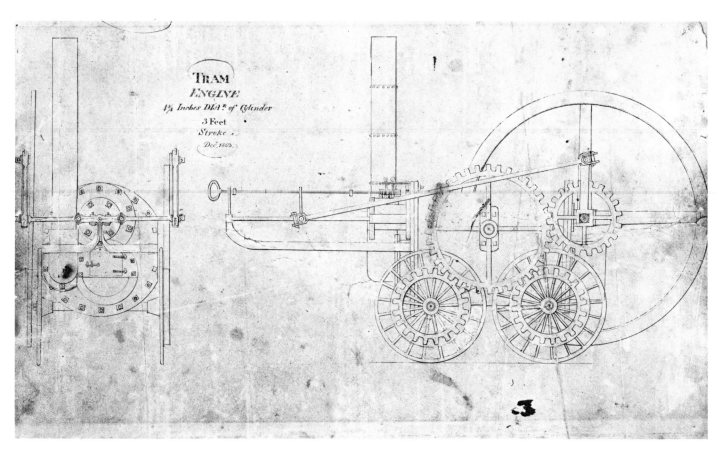

own experiments with a 'sun-and-planet' arrangement of gears. When the Pickard patent expired, Watt incorporated the crank into his later patents. In 1781 he patented the first rotary steam engine, which was used to drive a cotton mill.

In Fig. 2 you can see Watt's double acting rotary engine, with the addition of another of his inventions, the 'governor', a device which enabled the engine to be set to a maximum speed. It consisted of a double conical pendulum which revolved with the engine. As the speeds increased the two pendulums would fly outwards with the centrifugal force, and in so doing would pull a collar up its shaft. The collar acted upon a throttle which in turn controlled the input of steam.

The first portable steam engine

Several more improvements were required before the portable steam engine could become a reality. These were effected by Richard Trevithick. Trevithick completely eliminated condensers, allowing the steam to escape into the atmosphere, and reduced the size of the cylinders. This presented a problem, since the amount of power the engine produced was dependent on the piston diameter. So in order to significantly increase the output, while retaining small cylinders, Trevithick built a cylindrical boiler, which withstood far greater steam pressure.

In 1803 Trevithick mounted this very compact engine on to a set of four wheels. The engine had a return flue (the pipe that carries away the smoke and gases from the fire), which provided an extra heating surface and thus made more efficient use of the hot gas. The exhausted steam was led through a pipe from the cylinder to the bottom of the smoke stack, and with each blast of steam a vacuum was caused in the chimney making the fire roar. This method was later perfected by Hedley with his *Puffing Billy*, its nickname derived from the noise of

Below: An early engraving of Blenkinsop's rack engine, clearly showing the toothed wheel which meshed with a rack between the rails, giving the engine extra stability and adhesion to the track. (*Photo: Science Museum, London*)

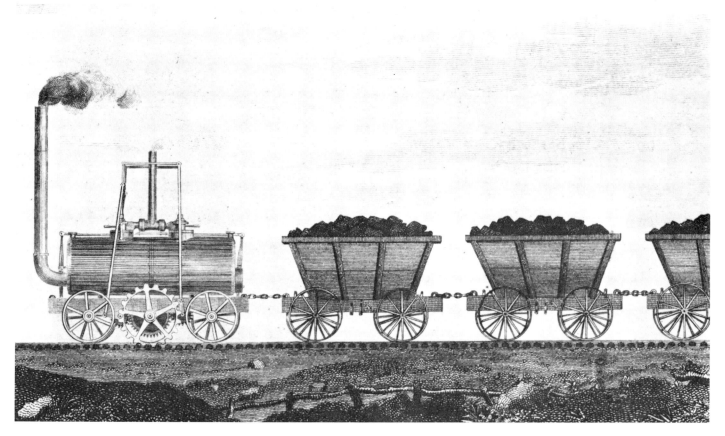

the exhausted steam fanning the fire.

The diameter of the cylinder was 2.4 metres (8 feet) and the piston travelled to and fro a distance of 1.3 metres (4 ft 9 in) with each stroke. The engine could move 2.7 metres (9 feet) with each stroke, repeating this 40 times per minute, resulting in a speed of 6.4 km/h (4 mph). One problem this engine had was that often the piston would stop at 'dead centre' of the stroke and would have to be pushed to get started again.

Trevithick's other famous engine, the *Catch-me-who-can*, dispensed with the complicated gear drives. The piston rod was joined directly to the wheels through a connecting rod, by means of a device called a 'cross head'. This was a universal joint that slid to and fro in a frame, enabling one end of the connecting rod to swing around the radius of the driving wheel whilst the other end moved laterally to and fro with the piston rod.

The rack engine
Within a short space of time the basic techniques of steam locomotion, which remained essentially the same throughout the steam era, were being researched and tested. Progress was by no means easy however. Engineers suffered problems at every turn. The biggest stumbling block was the failure of wheels to grip the track properly. It was an easy matter to increase the cylinder sizes and boiler pressures, but this was of no use if the wheels had insufficient adhesion to the rails.

John Blenkinsop, the foreman of mines at the Middleton colliery, hit upon a solution to this problem. He had the idea of the engine actually hauling itself along the track by means of a long linear cog, or toothed rack, that was laid alongside the existing rails. This was the famous 'rack engine'. The engine had two cylinders, so that when one piston was at 'dead centre' the other was just one third of the way down the stroke. This not only meant self-powered starting, but also ensured more even running. Blenkinsop also increased the heating surface in the boiler, because the rack and pinion device allowed the extra steam pressure to be translated into work without undermining the stability of the locomotive. The engine could haul a heavy load up a gradient of 1:18.

The *Rocket*
At the Rainhill trials in 1829 Stephenson presented his *Rocket*, which was characterized by its high chimney and the almost horizontally set cylinders. The distinguishing feature of the *Rocket* was its multitubular boiler, a bundle of thin tubes replacing the single wide flue through which the hot gases passed. By using this method it was possible to heat more water at a faster rate because of the greatly increased heating area. Although George Stephenson is usually credited with originating this design, some experts attribute it to Marc Seguin, a contemporary French locomotive engineer.

The 'Planet'
Stephenson's next locomotive was the *Northumbrian*, which refined all the successful aspects of the *Rocket* design, as well as incorporating the firebox and the boiler in one long barrel. This led the way forward to the Planet series of engines, built by many engineers, but principally by Stephenson and Hackworth.

Above left: The *Rocket*, the locomotive whose victory at the Rainhill trials in 1829 signalled the real beginning of the Railway Age. It is now preserved in the Science Museum, London. (*Photo: Science Museum, London*)

Above: Excavating Tring Cutting, 17 June 1837. From J. C. Bourne's *Drawings of the London and Birmingham Railway*, 1839. The work was under the control of Robert Stephenson. (*Ann Ronan Picture Library*)

Left: A train emerges from Primrose Hill tunnel, at that time out in the country though now very much part of London, on the London and Birmingham Railway. From a contemporary lithograph. (*Science Museum, London. Photo: Cooper-Bridgeman Library*)

Above: The original *Planet*, the first of the series, pulling a train on the Liverpool and Manchester Railway. (*Photo: Science Museum, London*)

The Planet was supported on a rigid sandwich frame (wood laid between two strips of cast iron) which made the whole machine more rigid when under stress. One problem with earlier locomotives had been that the current of air rushing past the train had caused precious heat to be lost from the cylinders, so reducing the effectiveness of the steam. So the cylinders were moved inside the wheels, behind the smoke box, at the front of the locomotive where they were protected from the wind. This was very convenient as it provided a short passage to the chimney for the exhausted steam and the cylinders have remained in this position on locomotives ever since. The Planet with its 2-2-0 wheel arrangement could haul 80 tonnes at 20 km/h (12.5 mph).

After the Planet came the Patentee six-wheeled engine (2-2-2), also built by Stephenson. As was pointed out in Chapter 1, it was in this engine that the shape which succeeding steam locomotives would follow became clearly discernible.

To complete the picture of the workings of the early steam engines and their successors we must look at compounding. The first 'compound' engine, that is, an engine with two, three or four sets of cylinders, was designed in 1876 for the Biarritz railway by Anatole Mallet, a Swiss engineer after whom much larger compounds were later named. In a compound engine, the steam enters the first set of cylinders in the normal way; after 60% of the stroke has occurred the steam is allowed to expand under its own pressure into the next set. Each successive set of pistons is wider than the previous one, with the result that the steam yields every last fraction of its mechanical energy as it continues its natural expansion.

Another point of interest is the story of the development of brakes on trains. After the death of William Huskisson at the Rainhill trials, it became apparent to all that brakes were needed on locomotives, and

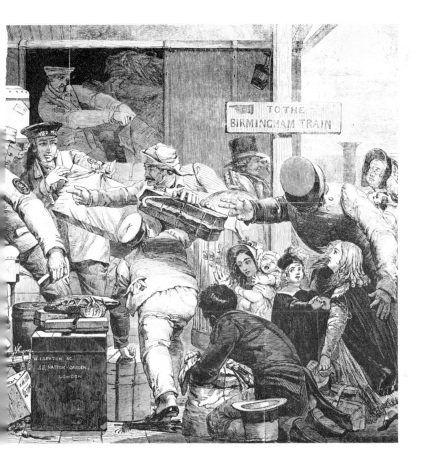

these were soon introduced. However it took nearly 40 years before they could be successfully linked to the whole length of the train. Many deaths occurred as a result of inadequate braking systems before public demand for a high level of safety eventually resulted in government legislation.

Robert Stephenson had designed a steam braking system, running the length of the train, but the system failed to work since by the time the steam had got half way along the pipe, it had condensed back into water. Experiments were then carried out in Britain with a vacuum system, which worked quite well but only if all the trucks or coaches remained coupled together. Then in 1875 an American inventor, George Westinghouse, came up with the idea of compressed air brakes. The Westinghouse air brakes spread around the world, but met with opposition in Britain, voiced mainly by a man called Webb of the London and North Western Railway (LNWR) who was paid royalties for the use of the vacuum system. Westinghouse has since become an enormous manufacturing corporation.

The Gauge War

It is often said that the tremendous momentum of railway invention and development in the nineteenth century was generated by the atmosphere of competition and rivalry. A more telling example of this would be hard to find than the so called 'Battle of the Gauges'.

The originator of the 'Battle' was a man whose name will always live in the history of both the railways and the Industrial Revolution, the British engineer Isambard Kingdom Brunel (1805–1859), He was a man of remarkable talent and energy who learnt his trade from his father, Marc Isambard Brunel; together they built the Thames tunnel in

Above: Isambard Kingdom Brunel (1806–59), the engineer who masterminded the Great Western Railway, designing all its bridges, tunnels and stations. Here Brunel stands before the chains of the steamship *Great Eastern*, his final creation. (*Peter Newark's Historical Pictures*)

Above left: The Break of Gauge at Gloucester, a famous etching of 1846 depicting the confusion and drama that ensued at Gloucester, where broad and standard gauge lines met, every time goods had to be transferred from trains of one gauge to the other. Damage and breakages were inevitable and frequent. (*Mary Evans Picture Library*)

London. It was during the work on this project that the younger Brunel contracted a chronic illness that eventually cut short his productive life. Perhaps his most famous achievement was the building of the Clifton suspension bridge spanning the Avon Gorge at Bristol.

In 1835 Brunel was appointed chief engineer of the newly formed Great Western Railway Company, and was charged with the task of building a railway from London to Bristol. This he did, and so began the period of railway history known as the 'Gauge War'.

Brunel set out on horseback, rode west across the virgin English countryside and surveyed the entire route in 16 days. He returned to his office in Duke Street, London, and designed everything that was needed: rolling stock, stations, depots, bridges and tunnels. Aside from the Gothic architecture that inspired the theme of the whole project, one aspect that made the GWR stand apart from other railways in the country was Brunel's decision to make the gauge, i.e. the distance between the rails, 7 ft (2.1 metres) wide rather than the hitherto universally used standard gauge of 4 ft 8½ in (1.4 metres). He had several reasons for doing this, the principal one being that he could foresee the technology of railways developing far beyond its contemporary level in terms of speed and weight of traffic. To have a wide track, he reasoned, would give future locomotive designers the chance of building really big boilers, keeping a low centre of gravity and still allowing greater speeds. He designed the coaches to sit low, between the wheels, but the GWR board rejected this as they wanted to have 7 ft (2.1 metre) wide coaches to pack in as many passengers as possible.

By this time several people, including Robert Stephenson (the son of George Stephenson and a great locomotive engineer in his own right), foresaw a great future for the railways, which encompassed the possibility that one day Britain would have a national rail network. Therefore they considered it essential that the 4 ft 8½ in (1.4 metre) gauge be kept as a standard, considering most of the railways were already that width. However, despite objections from all the other railways, Brunel went ahead and built the wide gauge.

The pattern of rail development at that time was that after the opening of a main route a number of smaller companies would be set up to run branch lines, or interconnecting lines between the main routes. This is where the main problems occurred. At every interchange between the GWR and any other line, all the goods and passengers would have to be unloaded from the standard gauge train on to the rolling stock of the GWR, or vice versa. This could take hours, especially when trucks were full of small freight items such as bricks or tiles, fruit or clothing. Thousands of pounds worth of damage was caused by the continual loading and offloading of these goods.

The other railway companies were of the opinion that if the GWR persisted in their spread of the wide gauge to the west, they would have a monopoly on the whole area. They therefore launched a campaign to have the whole question of gauges settled by Parliament. There was tremendous competition between all the lines at this time, and although the government preferred to leave it to the companies to fight out their battles among themselves, in the end the feuds were invariably settled in Parliament. By the time of the Gauge War the government already had over 150 Railway Acts under its belt. Therefore after much petitioning to Parliament by various companies, headed by Robert Stephenson,

Above: A landslide blocking Brunel's channel-side South Devon Railway track near Dawlish, Devon, on 29 December 1852. In the early days of railway construction accidents such as this were common and virtually an accepted hazard. (*Museum of British Transport. Photo: Cooper-Bridgeman Library*)

Above right: A portal of Brunel's box tunnel on the Great Western Railway near Bath. This beautiful tunnel is still in use and unchanged today. (*Museum of British Transport. Photo: Cooper-Bridgeman Library*)

Right: The *North Star*, the GWR's most famous engine, was built by Robert Stephenson before he embarked on his 'long boiler' designs, and remained in service until the end of the broad gauge era in 1892. Sadly this engine was lost forever in 1906 when it was scrapped. (*Science Museum, London. Photo: Cooper-Bridgeman Library*)

Above: This broad gauge passenger locomotive, the *Lightning*, was one of the 4-2-2 engines built by Daniel Gooch which hauled all express trains on the GWR until 1892. In all 29 such engines were built, on the model of the *Great Western* which had been modified from a 2-2-2. (*Photo: Science Museum, London*)

a Royal Commission was set up to decide the matter of the gauges.

Brunel put out orders for locomotives around the workshops of England specifying only the gauge and his requirement of high speed at low piston stroke rates. The engines that were delivered he found very unsatisfactory indeed, with huge 3 metre (10 ft) driving wheels. They all broke down time and time again, and they all had to be modified.

In 1837 Brunel appointed a young engineer named Daniel Gooch to run the locomotive affairs of the GWR. Gooch's first task was to renovate the existing engines and find new ones that were reliable. He discovered that the Stephensons' loco shop had two ready-built, but so far unpaid for, engines that had been constructed for a broad gauge South American railway. He bought them immediately. One of them, the now famous *North Star*, ran at 48 km/h (30 mph) pulling 110 tonnes. This engine was such a success that it stayed in service for over 30 years.

The GWR then had ten more 2-2-0s built along the lines of the *North Star*, and this model became the plodding workhorse of the network. Before the end of the broad gauge in 1892, a further 62 were built. One feature of these engines was that the spare parts were all interchangeable between different locomotives. This may seem obvious now in engines of the same class but it was in fact the first example of rigid standardization in locomotives.

In 1845 it was announced that the GWR intended to spread north to Wolverhampton. The Gauge War entered its final and fiercest stage. The Royal Commission was set in motion and heard evidence from all concerned. Daniel Gooch submitted figures on the safety and performance of the GWR. He was able to show that, whereas the major railways in Britain pulled on average 40 tonnes of passenger weight

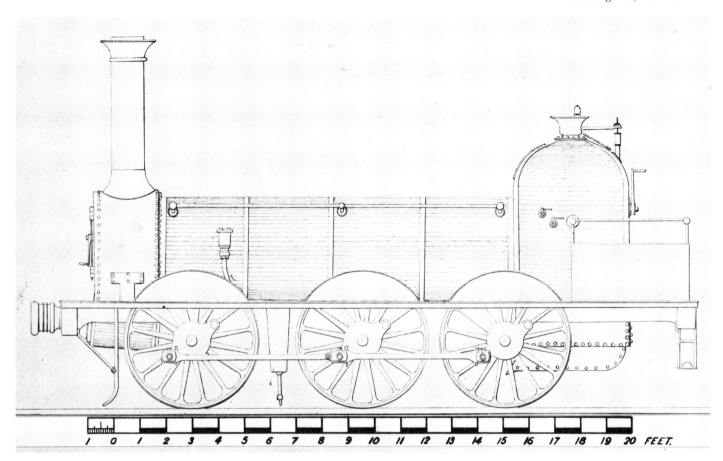

and 121 tonnes of freight at a speed of 32 km/h (20 mph), the GWR maintained a speed of 43 km/h (27 mph) hauling 68 tonnes of passengers and 269 tonnes of freight. The opposition was staggered, and immediately renewed their efforts to produce the improved locomotives that were later to prove the standard gauge's competitiveness, in speed as well as safety, with the wide gauge. As it happened though, their fears were groundless. The commission eventually favoured the standard gauge, despite the continued failure of the other railways to match the GWR figures.

In 1846 the *Great Western*, a 2-2-2 Patentee class locomotive, was unveiled at Swindon. It ran on the GWR at a top speed of 97 km/h (60 mph), pulling a load of 100 tonnes. Soon after going into service, the front axle broke and Gooch put two small axles in its place. The *Great Western* thus became a 4-2-2, and the first of the breed of express trains that served the GWR until the end of the broad gauge era.

The GWR began expanding into Wales in about 1855, but found that the hilly terrain posed particular problems. As a result the Stephenson locomotive works was commissioned to build a new class of engine, the Waverleys, or 4-4-0s. As with all new locomotive designs, no sooner did they appear in public than other railways copied them and other countries too. The 4-4-0s were most significant in the advance of railways across the United States of America. We shall come to that fascinating story later.

During the Battle of the Gauges the Stephenson works had been trying to match and surpass the performance of engines used by the GWR. Stephenson had no loyalties to any particular railway company, but he remained true to his belief that standard gauge locomotives could outmatch the GWR. Eventually his researches took him to the 'long

Above: Contemporary drawing by Lane of an 0-6-0 'long boiler', possibly of the LNWR. (*Photo: Science Museum, London*)

Overleaf: The 4-2-2 was a very popular engine all over Britain's railways in the nineteenth century, and the models introduced on the Midland Railway from 1887, sometimes nicknamed 'spinners', are considered by many to be the most beautiful locomotives ever built. This particular engine, no. 673, was in 1928 the last of its class to be withdrawn from service. It is now preserved. (*Spectrum*)

37

boiler'. He noted that when trying to stoke up and reach the speeds of the GWR, flames would emerge from the smoke stack, and parts of the boiler would melt. This he deduced was because insufficient heat was being taken from the fire by the water in the boiler tubes. So he increased the length of the boiler from around 2.7 metres (9 ft) to 4.6 metres (15 ft).

The first two 'long boiler' engines were delivered to the York and Midland Railway (YM) and the North Eastern Railway (NER). Alas, the 'long boiler' was still in its early days, and when the other railway companies tried to overtake the speeds of the GWR accidents happened. The 'long boiler' rode very badly, due to the overhang of the smoke box and the fire box; it would rattle around on its springs, making the ride uncomfortable and hinting at disaster with every stroke. In fact, so concerned was the government about this situation that for a time it considered imposing a speed limit of 72 km/h (45 mph) on standard gauge lines. This would have dealt them a crushing blow as it would have left the GWR alone to attain high speeds on its broad gauge.

The Gauge War was finally settled in 1845 when Brunel suggested to the Royal Commission that trials should be staged under equal conditions to compare the efficiency of the two gauges. The trials were held, and Stephenson entered a 4-2-0 'long boiler' which he had modified in an attempt to iron out its defects. The cylinders were mounted at the central point along the side of the engine, and lower down than previously, so that the characteristic 'dog paddling' motion would be less apparent. His engine was known as the *Great A*, being christened

Right: The *Liverpool*, one of many engines built by Thomas Crampton with the main drive wheel set behind the firebox to accommodate a larger crankshaft. These engines were especially popular in France. (*Photo: Science Museum, London*)

Right: The directors of the Great Western Railway lined up for this picture to bid farewell to the last broad gauge train to leave Paddington station in London, on 20 May 1892. (*Photo: Science Museum, London*)

Far right: The interior of the saloon coach specially built for Queen Victoria in 1869. There were many innovations built into this coach that were soon to be employed on trains all over the world, notably the toilet cubicle. (*National Railway Museum*)

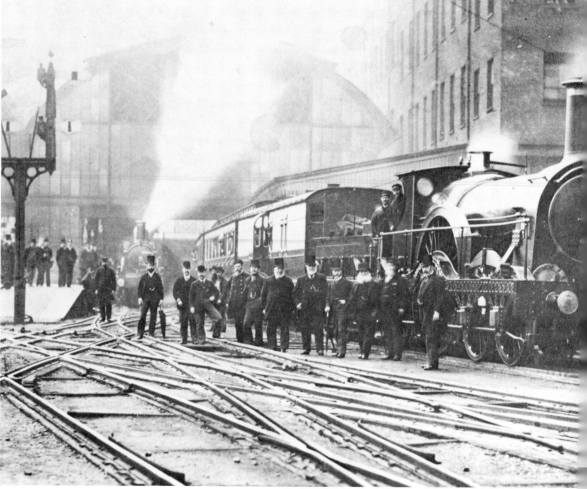

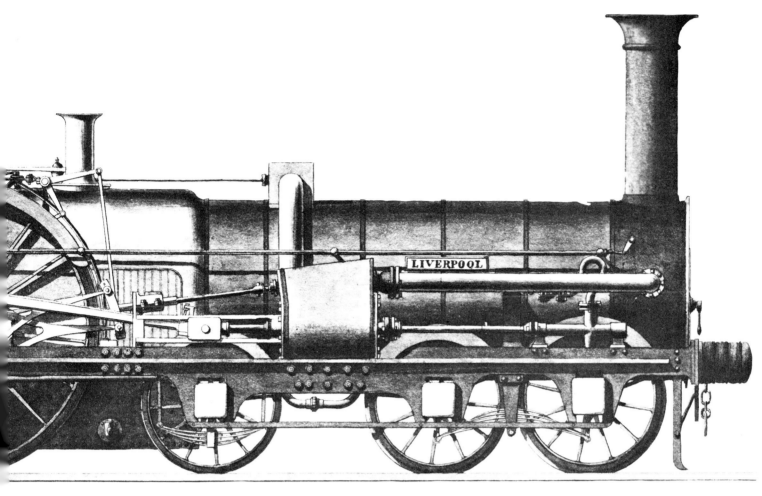

without any other name. Gooch entered the *Ixion*, a 2-2-2 Firefly class from GWR. Unfortunately for Stephenson and his supporters in the railway companies, the Gooch machine still came out on top. But Stephenson had now embarked on a course of improvement to the 'long boiler' which was in time destined to bear fruit.

Gooch had an assistant on the GWR, a young engineer by the name of Thomas Crampton, who had many unusual and imaginative ideas of his own about locomotive design. He had been trying for years to sell one of his ideas to different railway companies, but without success. Gooch was too conservative in his thinking to be attracted to Crampton's designs, and refused to try any of them out in practice. But Crampton in fact had the answer to one of the most pressing problems facing locomotive designers. He saw that one way to achieve a low centre of gravity was to locate the main driving axles behind the firebox, which together with the boiler could then sit much lower down in the frame, removing the problem of the unsteady boiler.

Crampton had no money of his own to develop this design, but eventually he persuaded the owners of a new Belgian railway, the Namur-Liège, which was still under construction, to buy two locomotives of this type to be named the *Namur* and *Liège*. In the event he finished the locomotives before the Belgian line was complete, so he tested them for a few months on the Grand Junction Railway in the north of England. Although the two engines suffered teething troubles they were able to reach a speed of 119 km/h (74 mph).

Left: A nineteenth-century lithograph of a train crossing the Crumlin viaduct in Wales, one of the many engineering achievements which marked the construction of the railway network. The railways inspired engineers to feats of bridging and tunnelling which a few years before would have been dismissed as impossible. (*The Mansell Collection*)

As the Belgian railway company had still not opened after Crampton had finished trials on his engines, he sold them to the South Eastern Railway. He then received an order from the London Birmingham Railway for a larger version of the *Namur*, which was supplied in 1848, and named the *London*. This line was in direct competition with the GWR on its northern routes, and the GWR realised that its hold on the speed records was slipping. In reply to this threat, Gooch built a new 4-2-2 known as the *Iron Duke* and immediately found it matched by Crampton's latest engine, the *Liverpool*, the design of which was entirely new. Crampton built the *Liverpool*'s extended boiler out of two half-cylinders of different size, the larger one being tilted on top of the other, which fitted low between the frames, in accordance with requirements for a low centre of gravity. It had 300 heating tubes, and was the first locomotive to be fitted with a regulator valve on top of the boiler. With these new features the *Liverpool* reached 80 km/h (50 mph) hauling 150 tonnes. That was the final blow. The standard gauge had won, not only in law, but also on the performance of its engines. The *Liverpool* became celebrated, and was shown at the Great Exhibition in 1851.

The Gauge War was really over. The broad gauge was eventually phased out over 20 years, the last train leaving Paddington on Brunel's gauge in 1892. The Stephenson works continued to sell locomotives throughout the world, although Robert Stephenson himself devoted most of his later years, until his death in 1859, to designing bridges.

Brunel also went on to many other triumphs of engineering design

and construction. Among other achievements, he designed the first ocean-going iron steamship, the *Great Eastern*. On the day of its maiden voyage, Brunel lay dying, anxious for news of his latest endeavour. Sadly, he had to be informed that the vessel had suffered an explosion and lay crippled at Weymouth. It was the last news he ever received, for he died the same night.

After the Gauge War

Although an Act of Parliament had forced the standard gauge on Britain's railways, the Great Western continued to use its broad gauge until 1892. It had hundreds of locomotives with the 2 metre (7 ft) wheel base which had to be replaced. In the process of phasing out, a third rail was laid along the track so that rolling stock from both gauges could be used.

With the death of George Stephenson in 1848, and Robert's withdrawal from locomotive design, railway's first generation of designers effectively passed away. Rapid progress was made in the second half of the nineteenth century. Many improvements were made to the style and comfort of passenger travel resulting from the patronage of the railways by Queen Victoria and Prince Albert. In 1850, the first lavatories were installed on the GWR. Heating systems, using steam piped from the engine, were installed in some coaches. In one of Victoria's coaches was a lever-operated signal leading to the driver's cab, so that she could indicate to him her displeasure at the speed they were travelling. Victoria would not allow any train she was on to exceed 48 km/h (30 mph).

The royal train that ran from London to Windsor Castle from 1869 had two coaches, one to serve Her Majesty by day and the other by night. They were connected by a flexible bellows corridor, an innovation at this time. In America George Pullman adopted the bellows idea and connected all his coaches in this manner, and the idea was later re-imported into Britain.

To celebrate the Royal Diamond Jubilee in 1897, the GWR built a commemorative train at a cost of £40000. Victoria travelled on it up to London from Windsor on the big day. Just over three years later the same train brought the Queen in her coffin from Portsmouth to London.

At the close of the nineteenth century, Britain led the world in the all-round operational performance of her railways. According to a survey made in the late 1890s Britain could offer 101234 kilometres (62904 miles) of express service at an average speed of 67 km/h (41.6

Above left: The London & North Western 2-4-0 locomotive *Hardwicke*, which in August 1895, at the height of the 'Race to the North', set a record by travelling from Crewe to Carlisle at an average speed of 108.1 km/h (67.2 mph). This engine has been preserved and can often be seen working at exhibitions and shows. (*The Mansell Collection*)

mph). The nearest rival was Germany which could boast only 29 993 kilometres (18 637 miles) at an average of 61 km/h (37.7 mph). In the 1890s Britain was in the so called 'Golden Age' of her railways. All the engineering skill and artistic splendour of the time was employed in making the steam railway a most formidable force, an experience that people from all strata of society enjoyed and used. The thrust of the ever-expanding system had moved more freight and greater numbers of people more quickly than had ever before been dreamed possible. The craftsmanship and opulence of both locomotives and coaches were strongly evocative of the Victorian age of privilege and confidence, soon to be shattered for ever by the onset of the Great War in Europe.

The two principal unclaimed routes in Britain were those which ran west to Plymouth and north to Scotland. In the grand Victorian tradition, both these routes provided the setting for maniacal races between fierce competitors determined to secure the lucrative business to be won.

In 1895 trains on the two lines to Scotland, the western and the eastern, operated by the London North Western and the Great Northern respectively, constantly tried to outmatch each other's speed to Aberdeen in what became known as the 'Race to the North'. Scotland had become a popular destination because of Queen Victoria's well-known love of holidaying at Balmoral, her Highland home, and the widely read novels of Sir Walter Scott added to the public awareness of the Highlands. The opening of the Forth Bridge reducing the journey also helped. So, night after night, the two companies sent their best locomotives rattling off into the night. On one of these night sorties, the contest became so close that the rival trains were only one minute apart at Kinnabar Junction, both averaging a speed of 97 km/h (60 mph). However, the train on the western route reached Aberdeen first with three hours to spare. The following night the situation was reversed. The owners of the GNR, convinced that they had proved their superiority, told their drivers to revert to normal speeds again, but the LNWR started the race again and thundered to Scotland at 101 km/h (63 mph).

The enthusiasm for speed generated by the contest received a jolt when an LNWR train jumped the tracks at Preston, killing one passenger. There was a momentary public outcry and the races were brought to a halt. Even the designated 'safe' speeds for express trains were reduced slightly.

Soon, however, the public and press forgot, and a new contest started up on the Plymouth route. The Great Western and the London & South Western were both vying for the same customers, who were mainly passengers from the transatlantic steamers. George Jackson Church-ward, appointed locomotive works manager at GWR's Swindon works in 1896, set about designing locomotives that would set an impossible standard for the opposition. He produced the *City of Truro*, a 4-4-0 express that received world acclaim when it established the 'records of records' by reaching 100 mph! The two railways pitched their fastest and finest locomotives against each other, until in 1906 the races came to an abrupt and final halt when the L & SWR boat train crashed near Salisbury killing twenty-four people. After these incidents, railway activities settled down. Most of the system had been built, and the steam brainchild of the nineteenth century had grown up at last.

Above: The train crash at Salisbury in July 1906, as depicted in a magazine at the time. This crash put an end to competitive races on the railways of Britain. (*Mary Evans Picture Library*)

Grandeur in decline

'Oh Mr Porter, what shall I do?
I wanted to go to Birmingham
and they've carried me on to Crewe"
Music hall song of 1903, composed by Thomas Le Brunn and sung by Marie Lloyd.

When the western world, shocked and chastened, climbed out of the trenches in 1918 and faced up to a new era, industrialized Britain began a rapid change that was to leave many casualties along the way. Among the hardest hit was the huge railway system of the Victorian and Edwardian 'Golden Age'.

The 'dependable' industries, coal, cotton, steel and shipbuilding, were overtaken by new technologies and foreign competition. Later, they were hit even harder by the worldwide economic slump. Until the First World War Britain had led the world in locomotive sales abroad; in 1904 she had sold two million pounds worth of steam engines. Within a few years British exports and design influence had fallen, giving way

46

to increasing American, French and German trends. British locomotive shops were sustained largely by exports to the Empire, which was a major customer for many years.

It was at home that the railways really suffered. In 1829 they had begun to win a battle against road transport. Ninety years later they started losing it again in the face of the sudden burst of road activity pioneered by the motor car. Against the new flexibility of the car and bus, railway passenger traffic began to shrink. Quite slowly at first, and then with increasing obviousness, it became clear that certain routes, especially many branch lines, were no longer economic. In the days of the railways' long-held monopoly, many lines had been built as little more than grandiose gestures, devoid of economic viability. These were now becoming a crippling burden to their owners.

The First World War gave the lorries and motor cars their initial impetus in popularity. Soldiers returning from active duty having learnt to drive military vehicles were eager to continue doing so. Many of them established road haulage firms, posing a direct threat to rail freight services. The development of railways had had a tremendous impact on the British way of life; but that way of life had been transformed so much and so rapidly, that, by the 1920s, the railways themselves had become outdated. Drastic changes had to be made if they were to survive.

In 1914 all the railways came under the control of the Railway Executive Committee which co-ordinated rail operation for the duration of the war. The entire population was mobilized for the war effort, a situation unheard of before. During this time the railways contributed

Above left: Railways played an important role in both World Wars. In this scene from the First World War soldiers wait at Victoria station, London, to board trains taking them on the first stage of the journey to the Front. From a painting by R. Jack. (*Mary Evans Picture Library*)

Above: The Midland Railway 4-4-0 compound locomotive no. 1000, the *Maid of the Midlands*. This handsome class of engine, first built in 1906, became very popular during the post-grouping era. (*John Adams/Colourviews*)

an enormous amount in moving troops to the ports and hauling coal for the fleets in Scotland. Much of the rolling stock and little used track was transported to front-line areas in Western Europe, where it was needed to reinforce the badly mauled local systems.

When the war finished, the railways had been run so well under the REC that everyone knew that the old days of free competition and railway speculation were gone. A period of 'rationalization' began. In 1921, a new Railway Act was passed in Parliament grouping all of Britain's railways into four large companies, still privately owned, but answerable to the Board of Trade. These four companies were: The London, Midland and Scottish (LMS), The London & North Eastern (LNER), the Great Western (GWR) and the Southern Railway (SR).

The grouping of the railways had some real beneficial effects. It ensured the survival of many smaller lines that would have had to close down, had they not been supported from the coffers of the more profitable parts of the network. The act allowed for a cross-fertilization of experience throughout the railway system, so that the entire network could benefit from mistakes or discoveries made on any line. Unfortunately, this led to the establishment of rigid policy standards which were often inapplicable in a given locality.

During this whole period of financial uncertainty, one rail system had continued to thrive: the London underground railway, or Metropolitan Railway as it had been called when it opened in 1863.

The new-found wealth of industrialization brought increased business and traffic to the centre of nineteenth-century London, and soon the streets became choked with horse-drawn carts and carriages. There were many horse-drawn buses, some of which were operated by the railway companies to ferry passengers between the main line stations. These buses found it increasingly difficult to be punctual, with the result that passengers frequently missed their connections. In response to this problem, a plan was formed to encircle central London with a rail link connecting main line termini both north and south of the River Thames. In 1863 the first section of this, a short line between

Paddington Station and Farringdon Street, was opened. Most of the capital outlay, which amounted to over £175 000, came from the Great Western Railway. This first section is part of the present day Metropolitan line, which also runs concurrently with the northern segment of the Circle line.

The engineering problems were, fortunately, quite easily overcome. The lines ran alongside existing streets where possible, employing a tunnelling method called 'cut-and-cover', whereby a channel was cut deep enough to accommodate a train, and covered over again at ground level. Of course steam trains were used initially, which made travelling on the 'underground' rather unpleasant. The mixture of steam, heat, smoke and sulphur fumes was reputedly a good cure for asthma, and for years patronage of the Inner Circle line was a recommended treatment for the complaint. Sir John Fowler, the GWR's chief engineer at the time, tried to improve the acrid atmosphere by designing an engine that used white hot bricks to fire the boiler. These were heated by small furnaces by the track side. However, the scheme proved impractical, and the idea was dropped. Eventually, people became used to the fumes.

The 'cut-and-cover' method of tunnelling was convenient for the construction crews, but caused havoc in the streets above, so engineers investigated the possibility of digging much deeper. The first deep tunnel was cut in 1870 to carry passengers, by means of a cable traction engine, under the River Thames. Twenty years later, a proper 'tube' railway similar to those of today was opened between Monument and Stockwell. Instead of the filthy steam locomotives new electric engines were used. However, steam prevailed for many years on the shallower lines.

The steam engines most commonly used were 0-6-0 tanks, although 0-4-2s and 2-4-0s also worked the lines. Nothing larger than these was ever used, as the locomotive size was restricted by the width and height of the tunnels. Steam engines remained in use on the London railway system well into the 1930s, but only on the sections that ran overground in the suburbs.

Just as the national railway systems began under free enterprise, so too did the underground. The Metropolitan line was equipped with the rolling stock of the GWR, using the three-rail system employed by the GWR for phasing over from broad to standard gauge. This was fortunate, as early in the life of the Metropolitan its board of directors had a disagreement with the GWR board, who subsequently removed all the rolling stock. The line borrowed new rolling stock from the Great Northern Railway, and was soon making enough money to re-equip itself entirely with new rolling stock. Later, when the Metropolitan and the GWR had reconciled their differences, their lines were joined once more and extended to Liverpool Street in the east and Hammersmith in the west. Eventually the Metropolitan line reached south across the Thames to New Cross.

Many more railway companies were formed, and London's inner system spread its tentacles to all the surrounding towns and villages, which have since become London suburbs and boroughs. Following the example of the London underground system, other cities followed. Glasgow had a cable railway built beneath it in 1896, Paris opened its first *metro* in 1900, and the first New York subway was opened in 1904.

Despite the rationalizing, the real enemies of the railways remained the private car and the public bus. Road haulage firms were set up, adding still more competition to the railways. The only way for the battle between roads and railways to be fought was in Parliament. The railways were the biggest single employer in the country, which placed great pressure on the government to curb the ever increasing advantages that road transporters enjoyed, and to invest in the railways. Road tax was introduced, and passenger duty tax was lifted from the railway operators, as was the land rate tax on railway property.

Unfortunately for the railways, these measures proved to be only cosmetic, and private transport continued to become more popular. At first the railway companies bought motor buses to ferry passengers between stations and town centres. But this did little to stem the tide. Small lines began to close, and services were restricted on others. Branch lines enjoyed a reprieve, brought about by the Second World War, until 1947, when together with the cross-channel ferries, hotels, buses and all other property and equipment owned by the railway companies they were bought from the 848 000 shareholders by the government for £1148 million. Nearly 30 years behind the rest of Europe, Britain had at last nationalized her railways.

Right: The Dublin to
Kingstown Railway,
Ireland's first line, viewed
from Blackrock. From a
print of 1834, the year of the
line's opening. (*Photo:
Science Museum, London*)

Railways in Ireland

The progress of Irish railways differed from that in the rest of Britain because the Industrial Revolution hardly touched the country until early in the twentieth century. Two events in particular spelled ruin to Irish attempts to build a strong railway network: the potato famine of the 1850s and the 'troubles' of 1919–22.

The first line in Ireland opened in 1834 running from Dublin to Kingstown port, a vital link between the Irish capital and London. There was a curious custom associated with this line in later years. Each night, prior to the Irish mail train leaving Euston Station in London at 10.40 pm, a postman would arrive on the platform with a leather pouch containing a watch, which had been set to Greenwich Mean Time. The watch was handed over to the postmaster on the train, whose responsibility it then became to carry 'the King's time' to Dublin. Although with the introduction of radio this practice became obsolete, the custom was continued until 1939.

The Dublin–Kingstown was the first railway ever to use 0-6-0 tank engines in regular service. Within five years the Belfast to Armagh line was ready to begin operations. Both these lines were laid in the Irish gauge of 1.6 metres (5 ft 3 in), a grand size indeed and an expense the Irish railways could ill afford. Later additions to the Irish network were sometimes built in a narrow 0.6 metre (2 ft) gauge, which was more realistic but of course entailed the same break-in-gauge problems experienced elsewhere.

Railways began to spread between major towns like Dublin, Wexford, Cork, Limerick and Killarney. But in the 1850s disaster struck. The potato famine that raged in Ireland for half a decade reduced the population, through death and emigration, to one-third of its original size. The basically agricultural economy took decades to recover from the shock. Industrialization had barely touched Ireland, and Belfast was

Above: A scene at Ballybunion, on the experimental monorail which ran the 14.8 kilometres (9¼ miles) from there to Listowel. The unique double-boilered engine was only one of the oddities of this extraordinary line which closed in 1924. (*P. B. Whitehouse/Colourviews*)

the only real centre of industry in the country. Nevertheless, there were still enough speculators with railway fever to ensure that railways did open. Most were foolhardy ventures, doomed never to make money, which often helped to destroy each other through the direct competition in which they insisted on engaging. At the town of Letterkeny, for instance, where the County Donegal Railway met the Londonderry and Lough Swilly Railway, both lines stubbornly maintained their own stations immediately adjacent to each other.

An extensive network was established across the northern counties of Ireland and down the east coast. The Great Northern Railway was the major operator in the northern counties, its lines spreading south to Dublin. But the war of 1919–22 and the subsequent partition of Ireland caused havoc with the rail network. During the 'troubles', the railways were a constant target for the nationalists. The Dublin & South Eastern had over a third of its locomotives destroyed or damaged, while the Southern & Western suffered damage to track on 400 occasions. This had a devastating effect on the already ailing railways. Then, when the fighting was over, new problems arose. The GNR rails, for instance, crossed the new border at 17 places, making it impossible to continue normal services.

The lines in the north were rescued under British initiative schemes, while in the south all 26 companies were amalgamated into one company, the Great Southern Railway. The GSR muddled along as best it could with out of date equipment and an organisation that was embarrassingly bad. The freight side of operations relied on the farming communities who used the railways to take their livestock and produce to market. When a scheduled train failed to arrive, a fairly regular occurrence, great hardship was often caused to the local community. Yet for a long time no-one seriously set out to improve this situation.

During the Second World War, although Eire remained neutral, she had great trouble obtaining coal to fire her steam locomotives. Many lines simply closed down until the war ended. Some enterprising engineers tried to run engines on bog peat, but without success. The main line trains would run only once a week, and when passengers did embark on a rail journey they had no certain idea when they would arrive.

Right: One of H. A. Ivatt's Atlantics, which were built between 1902 and 1910, thunders down the London–Leeds line hauling an eleven-coach express. These engines developed an admirable reputation as rough-riding, dramatic locomotives producing plenty of steam. (*P. B. Whitehouse/Colourviews*)

Sometimes an over-optimistic driver would set off with insufficient coal for the journey, which meant that, when it ran out, passengers and staff would have to leave the train and comb the local countryside for fuel before they could set off again.

In 1945 the GSR was taken under the wing of the Dublin Bus Company to form the Irish Transport Company (CIE). The new company then cut the railways by half, modernised the remaining lines, and introduced diesel locomotives on the 2400 miles of track still in use.

Ireland did contribute one brief chapter to railway history by being the first country, in 1888, to open a public monorail system. The line, from Listowel in Co. Kerry to Balybunion, was a charming and cumbersome affair, powered by a steam locomotive with two boilers, smoke stacks and cabs, sitting each side of the rail. It closed down in 1924.

British Steam: the last years

At the beginning of the 1900s Britain's railways were dominated by the 4-4-0s for passenger work, and the 0-6-0s for freight and shunting work. The new century, however, demanded that trains carry more passengers and a greater weight of freight to be economic, and these engines could no longer cope. A new generation of more powerful locomotives was clearly required.

The first 4-4-2 in Britain was introduced by Henry Ivatt of the Great Northern Railway in 1898. These 'Atlantics' used a similar mechanical design to that of the Sterling 4-2-2 'Eight Footers', but were much heavier and more powerful. Four years later Ivatt designed his own version, again for the GNR, which he named the 'Big Atlantic'. A total of 91 of these engines were built, of which the last ten incorporated superheating, allowing for greater improvements in performance.

When George Jackson Churchward joined the Great Western Railway he was faced with a wide variety of locomotives of varying ability. Rather than attempt to design a new generation of individual locomotives to meet existing requirements, Churchward worked on improving known locomotive design and adapting it to cope with the demands which he anticipated would be placed on railways in the future. This policy resulted in a two-cylinder simple 4-6-0 express engine, which he loyally named the *William Deans*, after his chief engineer. The following year Churchward introduced an improved version, the *Vanguard*.

By this time the de Glehn four-cylinder compound Atlantics had

Left: The *Highclere Castle*, one of the celebrated Castle class of 4-6-0s first introduced on the GWR in 1923. (*P. B. Whitehouse/Colourviews*)

Below left: The *King George V*, built in 1927, first and most famous of the King class engines which followed the Castles into service on the GWR.

appeared on the Continent, and Churchward bought one of them, called *La France*, for the GWR. Churchward liked this design, which enabled pairs of cylinders to be matched, thus eliminating the 'hammering' effect which two cylinders had previously produced on the tracks. His first version of the de Glehn four-cylinder was the *North Star*, but the success of his 4-6-0s led Churchward to redesign the 'Star' class using his successful 4-6-0 arrangement, henceforth the basis of many British express engines. From 1908 onwards Churchward also fitted his own superheater design.

Such was the success of Churchward's anticipation of growing needs that his successor in 1923, Charles Collet, had little to do but increase dimensions to meet new requirements as they arose. This resulted in the Castle class, which was still in production as late as 1950, by which time 164 had entered service. Collet further improved the design with the introduction of the King class, of which 30 were built in three years.

Unfortunately, their high axle weight prevented the King class locomotives from entirely replacing the Castles.

The largest of the new companies formed under the re-organization of 1923, the London, Midland & Scottish, introduced a new 4-6-0 locomotive, built by the North British Locomotive Company, to replace the engines it had inherited from its previously independent component parts. This was the world famous Royal Scot class, of which 50 were built. These engines easily matched the performance of the Castle class. When William Stanier became chief engineer on the LMS in 1930 he concentrated on standardization of design, even modifying successes like the Royal Scot class. One of his standard classes was the Black Five, which was built for mixed traffic, both goods and passengers. It was so successful that over 800 were built, making the Black Five the most numerous mixed traffic locomotive in the country.

In 1930 the Southern Railway, under the guidance of R. E. Mansell, reverted to the 4-4-0 wheel arrangement with the introduction of a new class, which became known as the Schools class. These engines were in fact the most powerful 4-4-0s found outside America.

Perhaps the most famous British high-speed passenger engine is the *Mallard*. One of a large number of improved three-cylinder Pacifics designed for the London & North Eastern by Sir Nigel Gresley, this highly distinctive locomotive, with its streamlined outer shell, broke the world speed record on 3 July, 1939, reaching a speed of 202 km/h (126 mph). One of the most exciting of all steam locomotives, the *Mallard* kept the record for many years, until well into the diesel era.

The Second World War limited activity, with the exception of the building of 'Austerity' locomotives. Designed by R. A. Riddles of the LMS, some of these huge engines with 2-8-0 and 2-10-0 wheel arrangements were influenced by the locomotives of the same type known as the Liberty class, built by the American Locomotive Company in the USA and used by the Allied forces in the war.

After the war, when the four companies were nationalized, another attempt was made to standardize locomotive types. Eventually twelve classes were agreed upon. Some were derivations of earlier types, but Riddles, now chief engineer at the newly formed British Railways, designed one last important new class of steam engines, the Britannia, a powerful 4-6-2 Pacific. In 1955, BR began introducing diesels, and five years later the last British-built steam locomotive, the *Evening Star*, a 2-10-0 freight engine, was rolled from the locomotive shops at Swindon.

End of the line: the Beeching 'axe'

Regardless of attempts by British Railways to trim operations and to make as much of the national system as possible a profitable concern, the roads continued to eat into their business. As the average wage increased and the population continued to swell, more and more cars appeared on the roads, so that by 1950 there were over 2½ million cars. That figure was to rise to 13 million within twenty years.

The postwar decline in the coal industry meant less freight for the railways. In 1948 about 161.5 million tonnes of coal were transported by rail; by the late fifties this figure had dropped by 11 million tonnes. In the early days of industrialization factory owners had found they could build their businesses away from their source of raw materials as long

Above right: The A4 Pacific *Mallard*, holder of the world speed record for a steam train, leaving King's Cross with the 'Tyne-Tees Pullman' express. Built in 1935, the *Mallard*, and all the other A4 Pacifics except one which was destroyed in 1942, remained in service until the 1960s. (*P. B. Whitehouse/Colourviews*)

Right: Riddles' wartime 2-8-0 'Austerity' locomotives numbered about 900 in all, and many of them survived for years after the war. Here one of them hauls a freight train on the Midland Region in 1963. (*Brian Stephenson*)

as there was a railhead in the area. Now it was good road connections that were important, while the railways increasingly lay idle.

In the face of such competition further attempts were made at re-organization, and for a decade until 1960 various minor changes were made, reinvestment sought, and electrification started on some lines, although the Southern Railway commuter service had employed electric trains since the late 1930s. A government Select Committee issued a report in 1960 recommending that the British Transport Committee should be replaced by a British Railways Board, which would have sub-regional authorities to prevent overcentralization.

A successful industrialist, Dr Beeching, was appointed as the new British Railways chairman in 1962. He began the painful process of modernizing the railways of Britain with the publication of his first annual report, *The Reshaping of British Railways*, in which he promised to cut back all loss-making aspects of BR's operations. Small villages and towns lived in fear of the Beeching 'axe' lest their local line be closed, cutting them off from the main railway routes. In just three years Dr Beeching cut the rail mileage down to 11500, a move which shocked the nation. Rolling stock was sold off and thousands made redundant. The British people, spoiled for years by the most saturated railway network in the world, had been little concerned about its unprofitability. They were unprepared for such swingeing cuts, and took the news of their implementation very badly.

The village station on its branch line was a door through which some communities received almost every commodity they required. Local produce was sent away to the town or city, and consumer goods were imported in abundance. It was the multitudinous branch lines which enabled a truly national newspaper service to be run and facilitated the national distribution of milk. It was usually local money that had built these lines as a matter of necessity or prestige, and strong local pride was attached to them. As far as people in many small towns and villages

Above left: The depressing sight, not uncommon during the 1960s, of an abandoned station on a branch line dealt the death blow by Dr Beeching's 'axe'. (*P. B. Whitehouse/Colourviews*)

Above: No. 70000, the first Britannia class Pacific, designed by R. H. Riddles. The first of twelve standard designs produced for British Railways from 1950, the Britannia worked the lines until the very end of steam. (*Spectrum*)

Left: The trackside notice foretells the doom of the steam train thundering past it. The modernization process instituted by Dr Beeching in 1962 ensured that within a few years steam locomotives on scheduled lines would be a thing of the past. (*Interfoto Archives*)

were concerned, it was the railway that put their community on the map. It enabled them to visit larger towns and cities, and allowed young people to go in search of work in larger centres without becoming cut off from their families.

It was therefore quite understandable that the extensive Beeching cuts hit the smaller isolated communities the most. Alternative bus services were provided, but these were often inconvenient, morning buses having to leave perhaps two hours earlier than the equivalent train would normally have done. The buses were not as comfortable as the trains either. However, eventually people had to accept the inevitable and adapt to the new situation.

One compensating side effect of the closures was that where a line had been taken up, an abundance of wildlife would sometimes spring up, in some cases ensuring the survival of endangered species of flora and fauna. In some city areas where lines were closed, the land thus released might be the only available green space, and local authorities were able to use it to provide rural walks and play areas.

Dr Beeching's streamlining of British Railways extended even to shortening its name, to British Rail. Other changes that made a big impact were the redesigning of uniforms and the introduction of the 24-hour clock on all timetables. The latter again drew much adverse comment, as people complained that its unfamiliarity forced on them an extra difficulty which they could well do without.

But perhaps Dr Beeching's worst crime in the eyes of at least some sections of the British public was to abandon the use of steam locomotives on Britain's railways. Although the demise of steam was inevitable, for many people it was a highly sensitive subject. Beeching, however, showed little sympathy for lovers of steam railways. In a recent interview he commented: "I'm not a cold blooded man, but I can't get all worked up about a piece of ironmongery". People fought hard to persuade Beeching to keep steam running on remaining branch lines, but he argued that to have diesels and steam running on the same network would require uneconomic dual facilities. Within four years all locomotives were diesel or electric, most branch line cuts had been carried out, and freight transport methods had changed radically. The new trend was towards containerization, the movement of goods in large sealed boxes that could be lifted from lorry to train to ship, replacing hundreds of men with two or three hoists. The first foreign container to arrive in Britain reached the port of Harwich in May 1969, having travelled 12 225 kilometres (7596 miles) from Japan via the Trans Siberian Railway to Holland.

The whole nature of the railways had changed during the Beeching era, from a widely spread service reaching into every nook and cranny of the British Isles to a fast, more efficient inter-city service, with freightliners (container trains) and company-sponsored trains handling the movement of goods. The railways' job was to move goods in bulk, not to offload them. It was with this approach that British Rail moved forward into the 1970s and 80s.

As Dr Beeching had insisted, there was, sadly, no place for the steam locomotive in this new railway age. On 24 October 1968 the throttle was eased open on a Pacific express engine of Western Region, and the last regular British passenger service hauled by a steam engine, the 5.40 pm to Banbury, crept out of Paddington station in London.

Above: The last new design of British steam locomotive, built in the late 1950s, was the class 9 2-10-0 freight engine. The very last to be built was the appropriately named *Evening Star* in 1960. It ran for five years and was then kept preserved by British Rail It still hauls enthusiasts' trains from time to time. (*British Railways/Colourviews*)

Left: The Britannia class loco *Shooting Star* pulls out from Badminton, heading westward towards Carmarthen in South Wales on a freezing night in January 1958. (*G. Heiron/Colourviews*)

61

How the West was won

'There is a great deal of jolting, a great deal of noise, a great deal of wall, not much window, a locomotive engine, a shriek and a bell'.
Charles Dickens, *On American Rail Travel.*

The difference between the expansion of the steam railway in Europe and the USA is that whereas in Europe the railways served the existing towns and cities, in America the very spreading thrust of the rails brought in its wake the building of towns where none had stood before. The story of the American railroad epitomizes the image of the old West; loud, brash, highly competitive and adventurous. In the early days the railroad men overcame mountainous obstacles, even beating off Red Indians as they built their lines. By the end of the steam era they had built the biggest, most powerful steam locomotives in the world.

How the West was won

Left: The Lightning Express trains leaving the junction, one of an enormous number of prints produced over a period of 25 years from 1857 by the famous artistic partnership of Nathaniel Currier and James Ives. This one dates from 1863. (*Western Americana*)

Communication in the 1830s across the vast American continent was poor indeed. It could take the Pony Express (a team of 400 mustangs and riders), changing mounts every 40 kilometres (25 miles) or so, thirteen days to deliver a letter from Missouri to California. It was becoming politically expedient to improve this situation as there was already a fear that territory might be lost to a possible Confederacy of states in the south.

Between 1820 and 1829 a few unsuccessful attempts at building working locomotives had taken place, but in 1830 Peter Cooper built the first running locomotive called the *Tom Thumb*. It looked much like Trevithick's first engine, with a vertical boiler, and heating tubes made from

Left: The *Best Friend of Charleston,* the first American-built locomotive. With this engine on Christmas Day 1830 Horatio Allen began a scheduled service on America's first operating line, the South Carolina Railroad. (*American History Picture Library*)

63

old gun barrels. The two cylinders were reclaimed from an old stationary steam engine. With Cooper at the controls it ran gently up an incline of 1:23, but quickly broke down. After a couple more runs it was discarded and never seen again.

In 1828 an engine called the *Pride of Newcastle* was built by Robert Stephenson and shipped to the USA. A couple of other locomotives were imported from Britain, *The Stourbridge Lion* being one of them, but all these engines proved unsuccessful as they were entirely unsuited to American requirements. Horatio Allen had ordered these machines on behalf of the Delaware and Hudson Co., by whom he was employed as resident engineer, and after his first unsuccessful attempts at buying locomotives he ordered an American foundry to build one. It was delivered in early December 1830 and called *The Best Friend of Charleston*. The trials were successful and by the end of the month the first American railroad, the South Carolina, operating from Charleston, was in business.

Sadly, the following June a bored fireman tied the *Best Friend*'s valve down, and the boiler exploded, killing him and badly burning the driver. The *Best Friend*, though, was rebuilt and named the *Phoenix*. However, another more powerful engine had been built by the West Point Foundry, from which it took its name – *West Point*. It went into immediate service and could pull 117 people at a gentle 19 km/h (12 mph). When the *Best Friend* was put out of action the *West Point* had to pull all the traffic on the South Carolina Railroad, so another engine was ordered, named the *South Carolina*. This engine faced both ways. It had two boilers back to back, and the wheel trucks were pivoted at the centre. This was the world's first articulated locomotive.

The lack of American industry forced the newly forming railways to import over 100 British and European locomotives between 1829 and 1840. Stephenson supplied many Planet types. These short wheel base engines worked well in Britain where the track was laid with care and precision but they rode badly in the USA where the platelayers had little experience or technique.

American engineers worked on the development of the 4-2-0 type, incorporating the same boiler and cylinder arrangements as Stephen-

Above: The *McQueen*, a typical 4-4-0 built for the Union Pacific Railroad by the Schnectady works, photographed at Wyoming Station in 1868. Perched proudly on the lamp is a set of elk antlers, a distinctive adornment of Union Pacific locos from the earliest days. (*Union Pacific Railroad Museum*)

son's locomotives. With the longer wheel base and three axles for support this type of engine was more suited to the irregular track. The original 4-2-0 was built in 1832 and designed to burn anthracite; it was soon converted to wood burning, though, as wood was by far the most readily available fuel.

The 4-2-0 enjoyed about a decade of popularity and was then replaced in the early 1840s by the 4-4-0. The first of these was built by Henry Campbell for the Philadelphia, Germanstown & Norristown Railway in 1837. Campbell's engine was a copy of the Stephenson Patentee class, but with the rear axles coupled and the front one replaced by two smaller axles on a floating truck or 'bogie'. The 4-4-0 not only spearheaded the advance of the American railroad; it became the symbol of the American West, easily recognisable by its ornate cowcatcher on the front, the wide spark arrester on the stack and the big lamp on the front of the boiler. This engine, together with its offspring the 4-6-0, became known as the American Standard, later shortened to Standard.

This engine was unique at that time because of the free-floating front wheels which enabled the train to negotiate quite sharp bends in the track. Up until 1900 nearly 25 000 American Standards were built in various forms by many railway companies. Engineers changed the size of wheels and cylinders, resulting in some very weird and wonderful-looking machines working across America, but essentially they were 4-4-0s as conceived by Campbell. Whether Campbell ever received the royalties he deserved on his momentous creation is highly problematic.

The original 4-4-0, the *Campbell*, went into service on the PG & N Railway in 1837, and could haul 140 tonnes up an incline of 1:67. For very slow freight work these early 4-4-0s could move up to 400 tonnes. They had a massive wooden frame and wood burning boilers. Quite apart from the wheel arrangements this engine very quickly evolved beyond recognition.

William Norris, who had pioneered the 4-2-0s, was quick to change his designs, and he became a key figure in the development of the American Standard. Another engineer named Mathius Baldwin, who had also worked on 4-2-0s, using a swivel frame with which to negotiate tight bends, also played his part in the development of Campbell's

Right: Across the Continent, another Currier and Ives lithograph, perfectly captures the pioneer spirit of the early American railroad as it pushed westward into the great empty plains of the midwest. (*The Mansell Collection*)

Below right: An advertisement proclaiming the grand opening of the Union Pacific transcontinental line, linking the Atlantic and Pacific Oceans. Dominating the poster is the Union Pacific's famous elk trade mark. (*Western Americana*)

design and actually paid him some royalties.

Baldwin began as a jeweller but in 1830 helped to open a machine shop making small stationary steam engines. In 1832 he constructed his first locomotive, called *Old Iron Sides*. In the 117-year history of the Baldwin Locomotive Works over 70 000 locomotives have been built.

One of the designs Baldwin produced was the 0-8-0 known as the 'eight-coupled' engine, the first of which was the *Atlas*, built in 1846 for the Philadelphia and Reading Railway. Instead of a front bogie, all eight wheels were drivers, and the whole suspension frame swivelled for cornering. About 150 of these eight-wheelers were built. However, they were abandoned in the late 1850s because there were so many moving parts connecting the boiler to the cylinders and valves that they were easily damaged in operation. Moreover, the side beams to which the axles were mounted were not rigid enough.

Norris built a variation on the 4-4-0 with a longer wheel base and added an extra running axle in between the two drivers. This engine was called the *Chesapeake* and went into service in 1847 on the Boston and Maine Railway. It was the world's first 4-6-0 locomotive, and the forerunner of the American Standard freight engine. The boiler sizes were increased after the success in the coupling of drive wheels, so that more power could be distributed through mechanisms which permitted a drive rod 7 or 8 times the length of the crank to be fitted.

Gradually the crude early 4-4-0s vanished, to be replaced by well proportioned and elegantly styled locomotives. One well known feature was the huge lamp that hung on the front of the boiler, costing 120 dollars to make at that time. With a parabolic reflector and French plate-glass windows the oil lamp could throw a beam 100 metres (300 ft) enabling the engineer to see obstructions on the line. Another feature was the cowcatcher on the front bogie. This device could throw a beast 8 metres (25 ft) away from a moving train, but by no means always worked – and when it failed there was always the danger of a derail-

ment. The railways covered such vast distances that fencing them in was impossible, and herds of cattle, wild horses and buffalo were free to wander on to the track. Railroad companies reported that while running through farm lands they could expect to kill 100 head of livestock each year.

Yet a third feature for which the 4-4-0 was instantly recognisable was the spark arrester on its smoke stack. On these early wood burning trains this was necessary to stop splinters from escaping. By 1840 three railways, the New York and Great Lakes, the Baltimore and St. Louis and the Richmond to Memphis lines, were forging west. Soon another line was started connecting Chicago to the Gulf of Mexico. The engines working these lines were 4-4-0s and 4-6-0s.

As the railways spread, the isolated settlers who had arrived by wagon train were soon joined by others who came bringing business with them. Towns sprang up everywhere. Sometimes stations were built before towns existed on the site, and in a few instances before the track had even arrived. Many early American railways were poor, badly built short lines, built by companies who had no notions of a national railroad system and just concentrated on running trains from one town to the next.

The 4-4-0 was above all the engine of the American Civil War. As early as 1859 the directors of the Southern Railway decided to build their own locomotives, but they lacked the steel works, and while they were being set up, the war began. The Confederate forces found themselves with old rolling stock and engines, with insufficient means of producing replacements, and with fresh supplies of spares in the hands of the North. They were at a distinct disadvantage. The North managed to produce or expropriate 300 engines which were brought into immediate military service. These enabled the Northern armies, of up to 100 000 men and 35 000 horses, to be supplied with as many as four train loads of goods each day as they marched inexorably towards victory. The South may have had all the good songs, but the North had all the good locomotives.

During the Civil War railways became an integral part of logistic planning, and were often a decisive factor determining the outcome of major battles. As a result each side's railway stock soon became a target for the opposing forces.

Perhaps the most famous rail exploit in the Civil War involved an engine called *The General*. On 12 April 1862 James Andrews, together with a handful of Union soldiers, boarded a northbound train at a station on the Western and Atlanta Railroad. Their object was to hijack the train and continue the journey northwards, destroying bridges and stations as they went. Andrews occupied the cab with a soldier who could drive the engine, placed the others in a boxcar, and ordered that the passenger coaches be unhitched. Off they went, leaving the crew eating their breakfast at the station. However, the redundant conductor of the train took up pursuit on a hand powered cart. He enlisted the help of a locomotive called the *Texas* and managed to catch up with the stolen train before Andrews had a chance to destroy any bridges. He and his men were captured after abandoning *The General*. A silent film of the same name directed by and starring Buster Keaton tells the story of this sortie in a delightful way.

The General was to witness one further round of hostilities. It has

Above: The *General*, a Standard locomotive which became renowned for its involvement in the most daring railway exploit of the American Civil War, pictured on a trestle near Louisville, Kentucky, in 1962, after it had been restored to run under its own steam for America's Civil War Centennial. (*Western Americana*)

more recently been the subject of court proceedings between the states of Georgia and Tennessee, as to who should have custody of the preserved locomotive. Eventually Georgia won its case in the Supreme Court.

After the Civil War the railways were in a mess, both in the North and in the defeated South, and the long slow process of reconstruction began. Most of the railways built up until the war had been concentrated in the east where most of the wealth and technology of the country were to be found. President Lincoln believed it would take a hundred years to settle and control the last frontier – that to the west, beyond Texas and Missouri. He was proved wrong, however, by the building of the Union Pacific and Central Pacific Railroads, a most daring and adventurous project.

In 1861 various plans had been laid to build a line from Missouri to the Pacific coast, and as a result the Pacific Railway Bill was passed by Congress in 1862. Two Pacific Railway companies, the Union Pacific and Central Pacific, were formed with the responsibility of starting the track from each end and meeting in the middle. The two companies were offered 30-year loans to finance the work with the additional incentive of being awarded a strip of land ten miles wide along the entire length of the track, in sections alternating from side to side. They were to meet at a point to be decided upon according to their state of progress.

The Central Pacific started at Sacramento in California and the

Union Pacific began in Omaha. The line was to take them over the Rockies and through the Great Basin. The project was expected to take 14 years but surprisingly was finished in only six, despite every imaginable catastrophe: avalanches, blizzards, bridge collapses, accidents with unstable explosives, and, worst of all, the continual Red Indian attacks on the work teams.

There was a great shortage of labour, and James Stourbridge, the construction boss for the CPR, was dubious about the growing numbers of Chinese labourers being hired. However, their loyalty and strength impressed him, and eventually his entire unskilled staff were from Chinese communities across America, and many workers were even imported from China. Stourbridge was a slave driver but his methods paid off. The Chinese managed to lay 16 kilometres (10 miles) of track in 12 hours at their peak of performance. Stourbridge was a puritan and forcibly removed any 'camp followers', whisky sellers, whores and gamblers, from the area. The Union Pacific was more lax about such things, and small tented towns marked the progress of the predominantly Irish team as it moved west. Two of these temporary settlements, Laramie and Cheyenne, remained when the railroad workers moved on, and became permanent towns.

As the Union Pacific progressed across the plains the Sioux and Cheyenne Indians fought fierce battles with the intruding railway, despite offers of free train travel for life. The locomotive was a mystery to the Indians and they were bemused when their arrows failed to stop

Above: A view of the ceremony at Promontory Point, Utah, on 10 May 1869 when the last rail was laid linking the Union Pacific and Central Pacific lines. The right hand side of the picture is dominated by the smokestack of the CPR's *Jupiter*, while facing the camera is UP's no. 119. Three companies of infantry were in attendance to mark the occasion. (*Union Pacific Railroad Museum*)

69

Right: American Indians attacking a train on the South Pacific Railroad in Arizona, from a French magazine illustration of 1906. Marauding Indians were a constant threat to the early railways, which were opening up for colonization areas where they had previously been left alone. (*Ann Ronan Picture Library*)

or even damage the trains. They even lassoed them, and were dragged under the unrelenting engines. Eventually they caught on and began derailing the trains by leaving obstacles on the track and pulling the rails up. The Army's response was to send 5000 men to guard the work-gangs. Sadly, however, it was whisky that won the day, turning many Indians into alcoholics.

The work reached hysterical proportions and the two teams became so eager that they passed each other, both gangs vowing to continue on to the other end of the route and thus create two railways! The government finally stepped in and called a halt to the proceedings. The two tracks met at Promontory Point in Utah on 10 May 1869. The Central Pacific had ordered for the occasion a 4-4-0 called the *Jupiter*, built by Thomas Rogers, an English engineer working in the east, and it had been shipped the 30 500 kilometres (19 000 miles) round Cape Horn to California. The *Jupiter* and the Union Pacific's famous engine the *119*, approaching each other along the two halves of the line, rolled nose to nose, cowcatchers touching; thus linking the Pacific coast with America's 48 000 kilometres (30 000 miles) of railroad.

The end of the Civil War saw the rapid expansion of railway networks across the United States, from about 48 000 kilometres (30 000 miles) in 1868 to 311 000 kilometres (193 000 miles) at the close of the century. Most early railway activity had been concentrated in the north-east and central states, but with the opening of the Pacific route a whole new vista of railway and economic potential lay ahead. This situation was exploited to the full, and steadily the population of the west began to swell. More new towns sprang up, new roads appeared, and three more Pacific routes were proposed. These were to provide an easy run to the west coast from any direction. The companies were the Southern Pacific, the Northern Pacific and the Sante Fe Railroads. Between the Pacific and the Mississippi River the length of railway track laid grew from a mere 8 kilometres (5 miles) in 1852 to more than 116 000 kilometres (72 000 miles) by 1890.

Left: New York's elevated railway in the 1890s. The railway was an inexpensive way of providing metropolitan travel facilities without the need for major engineering works. Later, however, New York built an underground system. (*Western Americana*)

This massive investment in railways was financially encouraged by the government in the form of grants of free land on which to run tracks plus certain concessions regarding trackside development. This aid was granted only on the condition that a railroad promised it would allow tariff reductions of 50 per cent on all Federal government and military business for ever. In 1945 a government study showed that a saving of 900 million dollars had been made for the US Treasury by this means, whereas the current value of the land held by the railways was only 500 million dollars, a considerable bargain for the government.

During this period of American railway mania, some men became extremely wealthy and powerful simply because of their dexterity in manipulating and financing projects. The owners of the Central Pacific and the Union Pacific Railroads set up their own construction companies to which would be awarded the huge contracts, worth millions of dollars, for building new railroads. These construction companies

Overleaf: The first journey of the 'Los Angeles Limited', one of the crack Union Pacific expresses, in 1900: the train thunders through the Californian desert. (*Union Pacific Railroad Museum/MARS*)

would charge the railways exorbitant sums to carry out the work. This left the railway companies financially crippled, while their directors made their own fortunes.

As the postwar steel industry got into full swing once again, the steam locomotive began to change. With the better quality steel available it was possible to build bigger engines, with more wheels and stronger frames. From the 4-4-0 came the 4-6-0, followed by a bigger version for freight transport, the 4-8-0. This first 4-8-0 was built in 1866 and was a derivation of the 2-6-0 'Mogul'. It worked well on high-speed short runs. However, the larger 2-8-0 soon overshadowed it. With the introduction of the 2-8-0 by the Lehigh Valley Railway the dual purpose engine disappeared. The 4-4-0 was relegated to slow passenger service. For a few years the 2-8-0, or 'Consolidated' (comically named after the Lehigh Railway had trimmed its operations to combat financial hardship), was the king of the freight engines. It could haul a 100 tonne, eighty wagon train at 23 km/h (14 mph). An example of its capabilities was the Lake Erie Railway's decision to replace over 100 4-4-0s with only 55 Consolidated engines to do the same amount of work. Well over 30 000 2-8-0s were built in America, some continuing in active service until the late 1940s.

The number of wood burning locomotives was falling, and by 1880 only 10 per cent of engines used this fuel. Anthracite dust, a by-product normally discarded, found a new job in the boilers of a strange-looking engine called the 'Camelback'. These engines derived their name from the extra long and high boiler needed to get a high enough temperature from a dust fire. Indeed the boiler was so wide that the driver could not see round it to drive the train. His cab was moved and mounted in the middle, sitting astride the boiler. Many hundreds of Camelbacks were built in the USA, working mainly on the eastern lines near the coalfields of Pennsylvania. They remained in service as late as 1956, although none were built after 1903 when a law was passed banning their production due to the many accidents in which the drive rods had come adrift and smashed through the driver's cab.

The demands placed on railways by industry boosted and enriched locomotive development, leading to larger, faster and more powerful engines. As the boiler sizes were increased to achieve greater amounts of steam, more wheels had to be added to distribute the increased load without extra weight being placed on the driving wheels. The Lima Locomotive Works introduced a freight engine fitted with a device invented in Britain called a feed-water heater, which preheated the water from the tender as it entered the boiler. The huge firebox was supported by four trailing wheels, and fitted to these rear wheels was a small set of steam pistons powered by the main boiler. This 'extra' steam engine gave the locomotive more momentum when hauling a long heavy freight train on its route through the hills of Berkshire, New England. The engine was called the Berkshire class (2-8-4), and with the addition of two more drivers became a 2-10-4 Texas class. Later models of the Texas could pull 10 000 tonnes, albeit very slowly.

Passenger locomotives also underwent major development at this time. The American Standard was still in extensive use, and one of these, belonging to the New York Central Railway, set a world speed record in 1893 by reaching 180 km/h (112 mph). But the longer journeys needed larger engines, and although the 4-6-0s and 4-4-2s had improved

Left: A streamlined Norfolk and Western 4-8-4 'J' class locomotive rounding the bend under Palisades, New River, in 1951, hauling a relatively short string of cars for its size. (*J. M. Jarvis, ZEFA*)

Above: The last of the really big engines, a 4-12-2, rolls out from Topeka, Kansas, with a freight train in 1952. Dieselization is just round the corner. (*J. M. Jarvis, ZEFA*)

the situation they were still inadequate. In 1902 came the answer at last: the Baldwin Locomotive Works presented the world with the first 4-6-2 'Pacific'. The Pacifics quickly spread not only across American railways but all over the world, and workshops in many countries began designing and making their own versions. The Pacifics' only failing was that they could not negotiate high mountain routes. In 1912 the addition of an extra set of driving wheels was found to cure this problem, and the new 4-8-2 engine was named the 'Mountain' type.

In 1904 the Union Pacific Railroad ordered a 4-6-2 that weighed 100 tonnes excluding the tender. The grate area was 4.6 sq metres ($49\frac{1}{2}$ sq ft), whereas contemporary European locomotives had only 1.9 sq metres (20 sq ft) of grate. Even this large engine was quickly dwarfed by the new 2-10-2 freight locomotives that weighed 120 tonnes, the tender when fully laden weighing a further 60 tonnes. By this time the locomotives had become so big that a fireman could no longer feed the fire quickly enough. The auto-stoker was devised, an Archimedes Screw that automatically pulled a continuous supply of coal into the grate. This era was marked by what was known as 'freight drag', when loaded wagons would be left for weeks in the marshalling yards until enough were collected to justify the use of the big engines. This practice ceased during the interwar years, when the railways realized that they had to find ways of speeding up the movement of freight in large quantities without losing the tractive power of the large slow engines.

Above: A 3800 class Santa Fe type 2-10-2 freight locomotive built by Baldwin's in 1924. These engines were so powerful that goods had to be piled up in the yards for weeks before enough were collected to justify their use. (*Santa Fe Railway/MARS*)

The final version of a long line of engines that had been designed to speed up freight transportation, was the Great Northern **Mallet** 2-6-6-2, which weighed 161 tonnes. This was an articulated compound locomotive which could achieve speeds of 40 km/h (25 mph) pulling 7000 tonnes. The engine's first six pairs of driving wheels, driven by high-pressure cylinders, were coupled to the rear six pairs of drivers powered by low-pressure cylinders, and the articulation of the whole gave it considerable freedom of movement when negotiating curves.

The ultimate solution to the freight problem was the biggest, heaviest, most powerful of all steam locomotives. This compound articulated engine was built by the American Locomotive Company (ALCO) and was appropriately named the 'Big Boy'. Only 25 were built, all of which were employed on the Union Pacific Railroad. Weighing in at 417 tonnes including tender, the Big Boy had the pro-

digious wheel arrangement of 4-8-0 + 0-8-4. The set of four free-running wheels led a set of eight coupled drivers, which were compounded to the next set, with four trailing wheels. The total length of the locomotive was 40.46 metres (132 ft 9 in), and it could develop 7000 horsepower with which to pull up to 4000 tonnes at 112 km/h (70 mph).

Fortunately, when at the end of the steam era many thousands of locomotives were scrapped, a few of the Big Boys were preserved, to testify to just how much ALCO's workshops had excelled themselves.

The passenger side of railway development centred around comfort as well as speed. The early initiative for better passenger services took place in the east. One of the first great expresses was the *New England Limited*, inaugurated in 1891, which ran between Boston and New York City. It was a most illustrious train, made up entirely of Pullman coaches. Each train usually contained parlour cars, passenger coaches,

Above: The king of them all! The Union Pacific Big Boy, the largest steam locomotive ever built. This particular engine, no. 4019, was the first of the type to be built; here it hauls a string of freight cars through Echo Canyon, Utah. (*Union Pacific Railroad Museum/ MARS*)

77

Right: The *Empire State Express*, one of the most prestigious trains in the USA, running through Dunkirk on the New York Central Railroad in 1952. (*J. M. Jarvis, ZEFA*)

a dining car, and 'royal buffet' smoking compartments.

The most famous of all the luxury trains was the *Twentieth Century Limited* which served the line between Chicago and New York City. The train was hauled by a Hudson 4-6-4 locomotive, part of the New York Central Railroad's 'great steel fleet'. Until 1893 both the New York Central and the Pennsylvania Railroads offered a 24-hour service between these two cities. There was tremendous competition for the lucrative business on the route, so that both speeds and comfort were constantly being improved. The rival to the *Century* was the *Pennsylvania Special*. As in the great races in Britain from London to Scotland, the war between the New York Central and the Pennsylvania Railroad was reported throughout the American press. The most spectacular story printed was of an occasion when the *Special* was running late due

to overheating. The engineer on the train borrowed a freight engine and attempted to make up lost time, and in so doing managed to reach the reported speed of 204 km/h (127 mph). This figure has been challenged as impossible, but it illustrates the fever that accompanied the rivalry on the major passenger lines.

The Hudson 4-6-4 had completely taken the place of the old 4-4-0s in American railway passenger work, and could be seen right across the country, together with a larger version, the 2-8-4. Both these engines worked the passenger routes virtually unchallenged until the end of steam supremacy in the late 1930s, and continued to play an active rôle until steam disappeared completely from the American system in the late 1950s.

The steam era came to an end as diesel engines became more powerful

and began to set a standard which proved impossible to match. Diesels were more expensive to build than steam locomotives, but running and maintainance costs were much lower. Steam had carried America's railways over the Rockies and across the deserts, and at its peak had worked a network of 409 000 kilometres (254 000 miles) which had required 1 650 000 men to operate it. But at a time when the railways were contracting anyway, steam locomotives were discarded by the thousand. By 1957 well over 90 per cent of both freight and passenger traffic was handled by diesel engines, and within a very few years after that the few remaining steam locomotives had all retired to museums, preserved lines or the scrap yard.

The other Wild West: the Canadian Pacific

As in the United States, in the early days all Canadian power and wealth lay in the east, mainly centred around the Great Lakes. Also as in the US the railways played their part in the westerly migration of settlers and fortune hunters and, most important of all, helped to consolidate the Dominion. The Canadian Pacific Railroad (CPR) was the country's main artery, forging across the plains and over the Canadian Rockies, and finally reaching Vancouver in British Columbia on the Pacific coast. The story of the CPR and the history of Canada are inextricably woven together. It is not too much to say that the CPR was directly instrumental in forming the destiny of the whole nation.

Canada became a Dominion in 1867, nearly 100 years after its dynamic and rapidly growing neighbour to the south had achieved its independence. At that time there were a few railways in Canada but, with most of the population centres grouped around the five Lakes and the two major rivers, the Hudson and the St Lawrence, most transportation relied on water. The entire population amounted to only 4 million, ten times less than that of the United States, and so the need for railways was less. The Dominion of Canada was at that time made up of four confederated provinces: Nova Scotia, New Brunswick, Quebec and Ontario. To the west stretched thousands of miles of sparsely populated prairie and mountain territory, connected to the Dominion only by wagon, canoe or steamer.

The process by which Canadian railways spread might well have been much slower were it not for the fact that many Americans saw the unoccupied lands of Canada as their manifest destiny, and the Americans were suspected of drawing up plans for the annexation of vast areas of the northern plains. The only way for Canada to secure her border was to draw Manitoba and British Columbia into the confederation, which she succeeded in doing in 1870 and 1871 respectively. The politicians realized that if Canada was to become a strong, united and progressive country a railway would need to be built connecting Halifax, the far eastern port on the Atlantic, with Vancouver in the west. Another consideration compelling some form of government initiative was the swelling number of new settlers arriving in the east from Europe. The railway plan became essential to transport the settlers to the virgin homestead lands, and thereafter keep them supplied with goods and equipment from the ports and industrial centres.

A decade passed, during which scandals and political problems cropped up almost daily. The project received a serious setback in 1873 when the scandal broke that the chief financier of the proposed Canadian Pacific Railroad company had also contributed heavily to the costs of Sir John Macdonald's election campaign a year earlier. The result was the fall of him and his government. It was not until his re-election in 1878 that the project regained any real government backing. The Canadian Pacific Railroad was officially established in 1881, and another great railway extravaganza was under way.

Since the 1830s there had been a strong interest in Canada in the possibilities of building railways, with many newspaper articles urging speculators to try their hand at building them. The first Canadian railway ran the 23 kilometres (14 miles) from Laprairie near Montreal to St Jean on the Richelieu river, and was opened in 1836. The purpose of the line, the Champlain & St Lawrence, was to facilitate trade between Canada and the United States. By the mid 1840s, with general prosperity and the example of successes in Britain and the United States, lines were being planned between many Canadian towns, as well as south across the border. Promoters in Montreal planned lines to winter ports on the Atlantic, notably Halifax, while the entrepreneurs in Toronto planned their routes to run north and west.

It soon became apparent, however, that without strong government support only a few short lines could be built, and in 1849 the Canadian legislature passed the Guarantee Act by which payment of interest (up to 6 per cent) on bonds issued by railways over 75 miles (120 kilometres) long would be guaranteed by the state once at least half the project was complete. This legislation was designed for big projects such as the Northern Railway which was to connect Toronto and Georgian Bay.

Above: The inaugural run of the Champlain & St Lawrence Railroad in 1836. The locomotive, an 0-4-0 built by George Stephenson, was imported from Britain. (*National Film Board of Canada*)

Right: Working conditions were hard for the gangs building the Canadian railroads. Temporary camps such as this, on the CPR, moved forward with the railhead every day. (*National Film Board of Canada*)

With the added impetus of this government backing many projects went ahead, and were completed by 1854.

The greatest railway project of this era was the Grand Trunk Railway (GTR), a Montreal to Toronto line begun in 1853, which was intended to be the Canadian section of an inter-colonial railway that would run through British North America from Halifax to Windsor. Huge profits were made from this railway, and the stock value of the company rose within a decade to $100 million. Enormous amounts of wealth were generated in construction, running and servicing of the new railways.

Canada's numerous rivers and lakes were a major obstacle to the rail routes. A large number of bridges had to be built, some of which were major engineering feats in themselves. The Great Western Railroad, which ran from Windsor on Lake Erie north to Toronto, needed a bridge built across the Niagara falls in order that a branch line could be run east to New York. The bridge was completed by 1854. Natural barriers such as the gorge at Port Hope taxed the ingenuity and technology of the early builders. The Port Hope viaduct was built by the Grand Trunk as part of its ambitious plan to link the whole of Canada.

By 1858 the GTR owned nearly 1600 kilometres (1000 miles) of track. That track left the public treasury with a staggering debt, while many speculators had reaped large profits from the project. There was a public outcry, surpassed only by the later scandals concerning the CPR.

One of the greatest achievements of the nineteenth century in Canada was the Victoria bridge that spanned the turbulent waters of the St Lawrence, linking the island of Montreal with the shore, a

Above: The bridge across the Niagara falls connecting the Canadian Great Western Railroad with the U.S. New York Central Railroad; from a contemporary French print. Finished in 1854, the bridge spanned 146 metres (479 ft). (*The Mansell Collection*)

83

How the West was won

Right: An early Canadian National 4-6-2 engaged in logging work. Most engines employed on logging duty were wood burning. (*The Mansell Collection*)

Below: The first through train to traverse Canada from coast to coast, hauled by Canadian Pacific Railway engine no. 371, stands at Port Moody, British Columbia, on 4 July 1886. (*Photo: CP Rail*)

distance of about 2750 metres (9000 feet). Three thousand men were employed on the project, which lasted for six years. It was designed to be high enough for ocean-going ships to pass underneath, yet strong enough to withstand the pressure of the ice floes at its footing whilst taking the weight of freight trains passing across it. The bridge was opened for use in 1859, thus completing the link between Ontario and Portland, Maine. The bridge was in constant use until it was replaced in 1898 by the double-tracked Victoria Jubilee bridge, so named in honour of the Diamond Jubilee of Queen Victoria, Canada's sovereign.

Many of the labourers on this and many other projects were recently arrived immigrants. Being poor and friendless they were ripe for employment as cheap labour. By 1860 Canada's railways employed 6500 men. American and Canadian railway contractors found that Chinese workers were more willing than European navvies to endure the hard-

ships of construction. Thousands of Chinese labourers were imported from China for the building of the Canadian Pacific Railway. Some others had drifted up from unsuccessful attempts at gold-digging in California, many of them having worked on the construction of the Central Pacific Railway on the way. Their reputation had preceded them to Canada and they were much sought after. By the time the Canadian Pacific had been completed over 16 000 had been employed. So began a racial problem for Canada that would grow to alarming proportions at the turn of the century, when the Chinese had become the scapegoats for Canada's social problems. Only in British Columbia were they welcome, where the swelling middle classes wanted domestic servants. The problem was not properly resolved until after the Second World War.

The next big project to be started after the Grand Trunk was of course the Canadian Pacific. It was so ambitious a venture that the project was divided into three sections. The first extended from Callander on Lake Nipissing to Fort William on Lake Superior; the second was the prairie section from Winnipeg to the foot of the Rocky Mountains; and the third was the final push through 720 kilometres (450 miles) of heavy mountain construction to Vancouver.

This last section was an enormous task, but the problems it posed hardly compared with those encountered on the section skirting Lake Superior. This section had to be carved out of the hardest of rock, and then further on, built on marshy areas that seemed to have no bottom. Often, great quantities of rock would be dumped into an area in an effort to give the track a firm base, and it would seem when the rails were being laid that the tactic had been successful. By the next day, however, the track itself would have disappeared into the swamp, and the whole job would have to be done again.

The construction on the prairie section was supervised by William van Horne, the general manager of the CPR, who announced that 800 kilometres (500 miles) of track would be laid within four months. He used 5000 men and 1700 teams of horses, and all but met his promise by

Above: A Canadian Pacific westbound transcontinental train at Glacier Station, British Columbia, in the 1890s. This stretch of track was abandoned in 1916 when the Connaught tunnel was completed. (*Photo: CP Rail*)

85

Left: Vancouver station in 1936, 50 years after the first transcontinental run. By this time 5 luxurious trains left Vancouver each day for the Atlantic. (*The Mansell Collection*)

Left below: A Canadian Pacific 4-6-2, the standard Canadian workhorse, leaving Montreal in 1952. (*J. M. Jarvis, ZEFA*)

Below: The ultimate in Canadian steam locomotives, the Canadian National Railways 4-8-4, pulls out from Toronto in 1952. (*J. M. Jarvis, ZEFA*)

laying 770 kilometres (480 miles). Every day, regardless of weather, supply trains would roll forward, each carrying enough rails, ties and hardware to build one mile (1.6 kilometres) of track. By the end of 1883, the railhead of the CPR had reached the summit of the Rocky Mountains in Kicking Horse Pass.

Throughout the following year and into 1885, work progressed at a good pace, despite interruptions caused by lack of finance, until on 7 November 1885 the last iron spike was driven into the track at Eagle Pass, in the Golden range in British Columbia, by Donald Smith, the President of CPR. At the ceremony van Horne made his famous 15-word speech: 'All I can say is that the work has been well done in every way'. The following day the first train, with Smith and van Horne aboard, arrived at Port Moody on the Pacific tidewater, the first train to traverse Canada from coast to coast.

A little more work had to be done on some sections of the line before the inaugural public train could run the following June. The first regular passenger train, *Pacific Express*, left Dalhousie Square station in Montreal on 28 June at 8 pm for Port Moody. The train arrived on time at 12 noon on 4 July. This was the longest continuous scheduled train ride in the world.

If building the railway was an arduous task, then operating it afterwards was often an even bigger headache. For example, at Kicking Horse Pass a 13 kilometre (8 mile) stretch known as the Big Hill was a nightmare for the CPR for over 25 years. There were stretches where the gradient was between 3.5 and 4.5 per cent, which at that time was the steepest rail gradient in the world. The first train to go down the hill lost control, jumping the tracks and killing three men.

Safety regulations on the Big Hill were rigorously enforced. At the top of the hill every descending passenger train would stop and test its brakes and standing gear. As the train then moved downhill, the brakemen would jump off at intervals and check that the wheels were not slipping or overheating. All freight trains were restricted to 6 mph (9.7 km/h) and all trains stopped every two miles at safety spurs. Despite these elaborate arrangements there were many accidents on this stretch.

The solution came however in 1907 when the famous spiral tunnels were built. These were carved from rock in the Cathedral Mountain and the Ogden Mountain. It took 1000 men two years to shift 575 000 cu metres (750 000 cu yards) of rock. From the east the track enters tunnel No 1, which is 1000 metres (3255 ft) long. The tunnel turns through 291° under Cathedral Mountain, passing under itself, and emerges at the opposite portal 16.5 metres (54 ft) below the level at which it entered. Tunnel No 2, across the Kicking Horse river and under Mount Ogden, is 900 metres (2922 ft) long with a curvature of 217°, and changes elevation by about 15 metres (50 ft) between portals. The spiral tunnels are still unique today.

The Canadian Pacific Railway, now known as CP Rail, serves all the provinces of Canada with the exception of Newfoundland and Prince Edward Island. It operates 27 500 kilometres (17 000 miles) of main line rail from the Atlantic to the Pacific and, through its American subsidiary the Soo line, controls another 7400 kilometres (4600 miles) in the USA's mid-west. Today CP Rail employs 36 000 men to operate its network.

Many of the locomotives used on Canadian railways were imported standard American 4-4-0s. In 1863 the Great Western Railway opened its first workshop, in which to repair engines and hopefully construct new models. Many of the skilled workmen were brought from Britain, and these men went on to form the first trade unions in Canada. The first home-built locomotive was the *Toronto*, built for the Grand Trunk in Toronto. It was a 4-4-0, complete with spark arresters, as it was wood burning, and cowcatchers. The wood was loaded from piles left along the track into the tender behind the engine. Often passengers would be asked to help in the loading.

By 1860 Canada had developed a considerable industry serving its railways. The Grand Trunk's Montreal yard and workshops formed a huge complex located at Point St Charles, where most of the railroads' hardware was manufactured. Most locomotive development followed closely on the heels of the Americans, with engines being supplied to CPR especially by the Baldwin and ALCO works. One engine, a 4-4-4 locomotive 3003, attained the official record speed of 181 km/h (112.5 mph) on 18 September 1936. This new lightweight streamlined train held the Canadian speed record for over thirty years, until well into the diesel era.

By 1954 the diesels had pushed 30 per cent of Canadian steam trains out of service. The age of steam was closing fast, and on 6 November 1960 CPR ran its last scheduled steam service. The event was marked by CPR by the use of a 4-4-0 engine built in 1887. The engine, No 29, pulled the train from Montreal to St Lin and back again. This engine is now preserved on display in Montreal.

Above: A 2-8-4 locomotive is assisted by a 4-8-4 on a tough stretch of track through the Canadian Rockies. Doubling-up of locomotives is often necessary when steep gradients or a particularly heavy load have to be tackled. (*Photo: CP Rail*)

The French connection

The story of the formative years of French railways runs essentially parallel with that in Britain. Some Frenchmen hated the intrusion of the 'iron horse', while others welcomed it. Pierre Larousse, compiler of the French Encyclopedia, stated that:

'. . . . a magical aura already surrounds the word [railway]; it is a synonym for civilisation, progress, and fraternity . . . . thanks to the railways, the birds and fish no longer have an advantage over man.'

The first railway in France was opened in October 1828. It ran the 16 kilometres (10 miles) between St Etienne and Andrézieux and was horse drawn in its first year of operation. Marc Seguin, the nephew of the

Below: A model of Marc Seguin's first locomotive, 1829, in the Science Museum, London. (*Science Museum, London. Photo: Cooper-Bridgeman Library*)

famous balloonist Joseph Montgolfier, had built the St Etienne railway, and in 1829 he imported two steam engines, built by George Stephenson, from Britain. The engines ran for a short while, but were unsatisfactory, and were eventually set aside.

Before the opening of the line Seguin had been working on his own designs for locomotives. He had been devising a method of heating the water in the boiler with a bundle of tubes through which the hot gases travelled instead of through a single flue. Eventually he was shocked to find that George Stephenson had been credited with this idea when he had incorporated the multitubular boiler into the *Rocket* at Rainhill. Seguin also introduced the rotary blower on locomotives, which consisted of two large bellows of the kind used to winnow corn, employed to blow air into the grate. The blower was driven by a belt connected to the rear axles of the tender.

The Seguin engine was tested late in 1829, just two months after the Rainhill trials in England. Known simply as *No 1* the 0-4-0 locomotive reached 19 km/h (12 mph) pulling a 17 tonne load. It was enough of a success to ensure two more orders for Seguin. He continued to improve his engines, replacing his bellows system with a blast pipe in the chimney as Hedley had done with *Puffing Billy*. As Seguin's designs evolved, the railway company dispensed with the four horses that had accompanied the first locomotives on their journeys, and pulled them when they ran out of steam. By 1835 12 Seguin engines were employed on the St Etienne line. A year previously he had left the company after disagreements, but his work on the railways continued.

From the outset, France had in mind a national network. Many of the lines built after 1835 were only granted a licence on condition that the railway would be the property of the state. The company would own only the buildings and the rolling stock, and after 99 years even these were to become national property. These stringencies did not however prevent a commercial battle between the families of Rothschild and Pereire for control of the lines.

Initially, rail development in France moved slowly, and by 1850 the country could boast only 3101 kilometres (1927 miles) of track, compared to 10 600 kilometres (6600 miles) in Britain and 5950 kilometres (3700 miles) in Germany. The French had little money or engineering expertise and were required to import all or most of their railway hardware and know-how from Britain. In 1843, for example, Joseph Locke, an English engineer, was appointed to build the Paris–Rouen and Rouen–Le Havre railways. Two of Locke's engineers, Budicom and Allcard, transferred their newly established locomotive works from Warrington and set up one of Europe's most important engine works in Chartreux. Locke also imported 5000 English navvies, who enjoyed the same level of notoriety as they were used to in Britain. The local French populace would make pilgrimages to the construction sites to watch these Englishmen work. They soon lost their popularity, however, when the Berentine Viaduct collapsed in 1846, shortly before it was completed. Nevertheless, the construction company of Brassey and Mackenzie, which employed all these navvies, had been responsible for building 75 per cent of the French railway system by 1897.

Initially France's gauge was dictated by the imported British rolling stock. The British standard gauge was 4 ft 8½ in, which when converted to metric is 1435 mm. The French at first rounded it up to 1500 mm, but have since reverted to the original measurement. The Paris–Orleans railway was equipped with two of Stephenson's 'long boilers' which were used for a couple of years, but not without the same problems of unsteady running experienced in Britain. The French locomotive shops then began to make their own 'long boilers'. However the French version had to have outside cylinders, because the home steel processes still could not manufacture cranks for inside cylinders of an acceptable quality.

By the time Crampton built the *Namur* and *Liège* for the Belgian line between those two towns in 1845, French railway companies were anxiously seeking an alternative to the troublesome 'long boiler' design. Crampton went to France with two more of his engines, which were not popular in his native country. He found a warm welcome in France, where his locomotives were used on the whole network for many decades, although he did not remain in control of his design. It was soon copied and improved upon, particularly by Camile Polonceau of the Paris–Orleans Railway. It was Polonceau who established the original French school of locomotive design. With his version of the 2-4-0 Polonceau tried to produce a locomotive for mixed traffic; later he tried an 0-4-2 with the same object. His most successful locomotive was the six-coupled freight engine first built in 1856; many engines of this type did sterling service on French railways, the last one being scrapped only in 1939.

In 1843 the French and Belgian systems agreed to connect their lines by running a route from Antwerp to Mons. In the same year Belgium and Germany were joined by rail. This was not a new idea; as early as 1802 it had been suggested to Napoleon that Britain and France be joined by means of the infamous Channel Tunnel, and work actually began on the project in 1881. It was to have cost £120 million to dig the tunnel 18 metres (60 ft) below the sea bed. The two countries fell out in the late 1880s, and despite the fact that the tunnel already reached a mile from the coast on both sides of the Channel, the project was scrapped. The costs had soared to a staggering £1000 million, and the idea was never pursued so seriously again.

In 1857, with vast amounts of Italian money, work began at Mont Cenis on the first Alpine tunnel, later known as the Fréjus Tunnel. This was to be part of a railway running through the Alps to connect Paris with Turin and Milan. Once completed the tunnel was 13 kilometres (8 miles) long, running 900 metres (3000 feet) beneath the mountains. No one expected the work to be finished before the 1880s, but with the sudden arrival of two very important inventions the job was greatly accelerated. The pneumatic drill and Nobel's dynamite enabled the tunnel to be completed by 1871, and the line was opened in the same year. Incidentally, it was the news that tubes of compressed air more than 800 metres (half a mile) long were working the drills in the tunnel construction that led George Westinghouse to invent the compressed air brake.

The following year the coastal route through Nice and Monte Carlo was opened, connecting France with Italy. It was this rail route that established the area as an international holiday resort for the genteel classes of France and England. The route also became an important lifeline between Britain and her colonies. Mail, shipped across the Channel, was carried on a daily mail train from Calais to Marseilles,

Above right: A contemporary print of the line between Paris and St. Germain, built by James Rothschild in 1837. The banking family of Rothschild built up a vast railway empire which covered much of Europe in the nineteenth century. (*Mary Evans Picture Library*)

Right: One of Crampton's 4-2-0 locomotives, with the distinctive large rear driving wheels, in service on a French railway. Crampton's locomotives, never highly regarded in England, became very popular in France. (*Mary Evans Picture Library*)

where letters and documents were loaded on to ships, gaining several days on old-established routes. It was also now possible to leave Victoria Station in London on a Friday night and arrive at the Adriatic port of Brindisi by Sunday afternoon. This train service was advertised as the *Peninsular Express*.

An important European development inspired by events in America occurred at about this time. A Belgian engineer named George Nagelmackers, impressed by the achievements of Pullman in persuading more than 100 American railroads to haul his luxury coaches, decided in 1869 to try to apply the same approach to European travel. He had five sleeping cars built in Vienna to his design. Each of the 8.8 metre (29 ft) cars had a central compartment containing lavatory facilities connected with three other compartments each of which could be used as a sitting room by day and converted to a comfortable sleeping room by night. Nagelmackers wanted to run his coaches on the *Peninsular* run, but the railway refused on the grounds that it would be expected to charge less for carrying mail if the train also took passengers. So Nagelmackers ran his first concessions on the Paris–Vienna service instead. In 1876 he raised 11 million francs and set up the Compagnie Internationale des Wagons-Lits, which over a few years acquired a reputation equal to that of the Pullman Car Company of America. Wagons-Lits, based in Brussels and operating from Paris, Milan and Berlin, were awarded over twenty contracts to operate luxury trains all over Europe.

Anatole Mallet, a Swiss-born engineer, was the father of the compound locomotive, which until electrification in the 1930s dominated the French railway scene. Mallet's first compound, which he built in

Left: French newspapers and popular journals often contained sensational depictions of railway tragedies, such as this one from *Le Petit Journal* of 1910. (*Mary Evans Picture Library*)

Above: A double-decked railway coach, built in 1883 and used on the Est railway. Double-decked coaches found favour in France, and are today used extensively on Paris suburban lines. (*La Vie du Rail*)

1876, was an 0-4-2 two-cylinder tank engine called the *Anglet*, which ran on the Bayonne–Biarritz line where it demonstrated fuel savings of 25 per cent. Unfortunately Mallet had trouble selling the idea to the big French railway companies; but his work did not go unnoticed. At this time Alfred de Glehn, an English engineer working for the Nord Railway, was trying to replace redundant and damaged locomotives and decided to experiment with compounding. His first attempt was derailed early in its career. He tried again, but with poor results, and so turned his attention to a 4-4-0, with two inside and two outside cylinders. This engine worked well, and de Glehn built two more such engines in Alsace in 1891. Both ran from Paris to Amiens at a steady 87 km/h (54 mph) pulling a 212-tonne train.

This powerful engine was given a further improvement with the addition of an extra set of wheels under the enlarged firebox. The result was the 'Atlantic' class, which appeared just in time for the Paris World Fair in 1900. This locomotive could pull 300 tonnes up hill at 60 mph (97 km/h). It quickly spread to most French railways, and became the main French express engine.

De Glehn went on to develop the 'Pacific' class by adding another set of driving wheels to produce a 4-6-2 locomotive. The Pacific proved very disappointing to de Glehn, for although it could achieve 38 per cent more steam, it could only generate 2000 horsepower compared to the

1800 hp of the Atlantic. However, engineers in other countries had much more success with the Pacific.

The compound, although also widely used in America, was characteristic of French railways. These powerful locomotives required an extremely high standard of footplate engineering. Each driver was awarded his engine for life and took ultimate responsibility for its well being and maintenance. This was known as the *machine titulaire* arrangement.

Many years later, André Chapelon, assistant chief engineer on the Paris–Orleans line, began improving the Pacifics on which de Glehn had given up. Chapelon felt that they were not fundamentally bad, and by the time he had enlarged and internally streamlined the steam passages, added a new exhaust system, devised by himself, and made a number of other modifications, the power output had increased by 50 per cent. He later rebuilt some Pacifics into 4-8-0s and achieved a doubled output of 4000 hp, from an engine weighing only 105 tonnes. Chapelon, one of the greatest of all locomotive engineers, continually improved upon his own standards, until in 1942 he produced arguably the finest steam locomotive ever built, a three-cylinder compound 4-8-4 engine capable of achieving 5500hp.

When one thinks of French railways the train that invariably comes to mind is the *Orient Express*. This train perhaps more than any other has fired the imagination of cinema audiences and readers of suspense novels the world over. Above all it is immortalized in Agatha Christie's *Murder on the Orient Express*, which depicts a luxurious, dark and mysterious train, as indeed in appearance it was, sawing and rattling through the night across borders hidden by snow. The passengers, apparently, all have a story of their own, each with a dramatic reason for being on the train, and most are lucky to reach their destination, having survived murder plots and kidnap attempts.

Opposite: The interior of the *Orient Express*. The first class dining car was decorated and furnished in the very height of Wagons-Lit luxury. (*Mary Evans Picture Library*)

Below: A nineteenth-century print of the *Orient Express*, from the French magazine *La Nature*. (*Mary Evans Picture Library*)

Right: The 4-6-2 de Glehn express locomotive. Built in 1908 and used on the Paris–Orleans line, this was Europe's first class of Pacific engines. (La Vie du Rail)

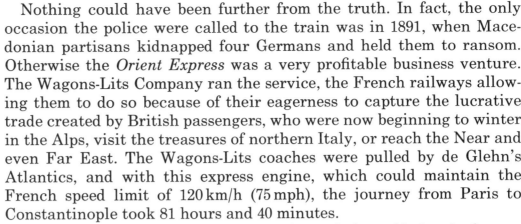

Below: This locomotive, a 4-6-4 4-cylinder compound, was one of André Chapelon's greatest designs. Twenty such engines were built, the first appearing in 1936, and were used mainly on the Nord lines. (La Vie du Rail)

Nothing could have been further from the truth. In fact, the only occasion the police were called to the train was in 1891, when Macedonian partisans kidnapped four Germans and held them to ransom. Otherwise the *Orient Express* was a very profitable business venture. The Wagons-Lits Company ran the service, the French railways allowing them to do so because of their eagerness to capture the lucrative trade created by British passengers, who were now beginning to winter in the Alps, visit the treasures of northern Italy, or reach the Near and even Far East. The Wagons-Lits coaches were pulled by de Glehn's Atlantics, and with this express engine, which could maintain the French speed limit of 120 km/h (75 mph), the journey from Paris to Constantinople took 81 hours and 40 minutes.

This incredibly long journey was only made bearable by the luxury coaches of the Wagons-Lits. These elegantly decorated coaches had cut-glass oil lamps, heating, and expensive upholstery, with a varnished teak and mahogany wood finish throughout. The original route took the *Orient Express* through Munich, then to Vienna and on to Budapest, where there was a change of trains. The journey continued for another 9 hours to the port of Varna on the edge of the Black Sea, from where the passengers caught a steamer to Constantinople. It was not until a bridge was built over the Danube that the through journey to the Black Sea coast could be made without a change of trains. The fare was £58 inclusive of any hotels. The journey was made even more bearable by the introduction of toilet cubicles on the train, and also of the restaurant car in the late 1880s.

The *Orient Express* crossed six countries and in intrigue-ridden late nineteenth-century Europe there was always likely to be an atmosphere of tension between at least two of them; something which may have contributed to the air of mystery which came to surround the train. Diplomats, couriers, businessmen and lesser members of the European royal families would travel on the route on both public and private business. This atmosphere of intrigue and suspicion was at its height during the days leading up to the outbreak of the Second World War, when the train's route was chequered with frontiers soon to be overthrown, in some cases for ever. It was an unnerving situation, and by 1940 the *Orient Express* had stopped running. The service was reintroduced after the war, but its halcyon days had passed.

It is arguable that the age of steam as a whole would have lasted longer in France, and indeed in much of Europe, had it not been for the two crippling wars, despite the well-laid plans of the SNCF (French National Railways) for the electrification of the whole network. The first trains to be hit by the outbreak of war in 1914 were the Wagons-Lits. With the occupation of Belgium the company was cut off from its headquarters, and with the subsequent collapse of the services that it was running across Europe international rail travel ceased.

About 3000 French trains were used for the mobilization of troops in 1914. During the first months of the war it took 400 trains to move the French armies to the front line, and another 350 to transport the British Expeditionary Force. Seventy thousand Ghurkas and Sikhs, brought across to France with all their equipment in 52 troop ships, required another 400 trains. Combatting the continued German offensive at Verdun required more than $1\frac{1}{2}$ million men who were transported, with their supplies, in a staggering 3500 trains.

Above left: From the splendid twilight of French steam: the Clermont-Ferrand to Paris express hurtles up the line in 1966. (*Marcel Aubert/Colourviews*)

Left: Two 4-6-0 locomotives pictured in the Paris yards in 1938. The decimation which French railways were soon to suffer in the Second World War helped to hasten the demise of the steam train in France. (*Colourviews*)

Understandably, within a year the French railways were crippled, hundreds of locomotives had been destroyed or severely damaged, and a complete collapse was only averted with the help of Britain. One thousand British locomotives were sent, together with rolling stock, across the Channel and rails that were little used in Britain were torn up and shipped to France. When the war ended, not only had the French rail system suffered the loss of countless locomotives and wagons, but thousands of men with the skill and experience needed to build and run railways had been killed.

The final blow to steam railways in France came with the Second World War. Not a single country in Europe had a decent railway left by the end of the war. The SNCF enlisted the help of the American

Above: In this photograph taken just after the end of the First World War, French mechanics examine a locomotive damaged during the war. Both world wars took a heavy toll not only on the railway system itself but also on the men who ran it. (*The Mansell Collection*)

Above: An articulated tank engine picks up passengers at St Julien near the Swiss border, on the narrow gauge Vivarais line in 1968. (*J. M. Jarvis, ZEFA*)

Baldwin Locomotive Works in replenishing stocks, and it supplied over 1000 2-8-2 engines which were all in service by 1947. They were for mixed traffic, and were capable of pulling 650 tonnes at about 97 km/h (60 mph).

Although no more big engines were built in France, there were two existing locomotives that were modernized under the direction of Chapelon. One was the 4-8-4 three-cylinder compound, converted from a 4-8-2 four-cylinder model. The other was a de Glehn 2-10-0 which Chapelon changed into a 2-12-0 six-cylinder compound for freight work. Both engines, however, were made redundant by the steady increase after the war in electric, diesel and gas turbine locomotives. Within a few years all steam engines, large and small, had vanished from the French lines.

Left: A powerful 2-8-4 locomotive of SNCF. Towards the end of the steam era France produced some of the most impressive steam locomotives ever built. (*P. B. Whitehouse/ Colourviews*)

The steam trains of Germany

Germany was a very late arrival on the railway scene considering her close proximity to France, Belgium and Britain. The main reason for this was that nineteenth-century Germany was still only a collection of small independent states, under the continual domination of Prussia in the north. Each state had its own government, currency and customs laws, which made it very difficult for any one state to plan a rail link across the country.

The first German railway was laid in Bavaria in the south-east of the country, and was named the Ludwigsbahn in honour of the King of Bavaria, who had been very active in promoting it. Opened in 1835 it ran the 8 kilometres (5 miles) from Nüremberg to Fürth, and was powered by an engine called *Der Adler* (*The Eagle*) which had been built by George Stephenson in Britain. The *Adler*, when it was delivered, was accompanied by its driver, William Wilson, the only man in Germany who knew how to drive the new 'iron horse'. Wilson was held in such high esteem that he was paid more money than the chairman of the railway company. He intended to stay in Germany only a short time, but he must have been gratified by the attention he received, as he learned German and ended up staying for 27 years.

The opening of the Nüremberg–Fürth line caused the Prussians to be very suspicious and distrustful of the steam engine. The following year Saxony opened its first section, from Leipzig to Dresden, using a Samson type engine, also from Britain. In 1839 this line was extended, and for the opening ceremony the first German-built locomotive was rolled out, the *Saxonia*, built by Johan Schubert following the style of Edward Bury's *Copperknob*. The Leipzig–Dresden railway carried 412 000 passengers during its first full year of operation.

The Prussian authorities thus felt forced to pass a Railway Act in 1838, so as not to lose step with states which they wished to dominate. This Act enabled the Potsdam–Berlin railway to be constructed. The Act offered no financial assistance to potential railway companies, and even empowered the state to compulsorily purchase the line after 30 years. Naturally, under these terms Prussia expected no immediate rush to construct new routes. One result of this lack of state enthusiasm was that the companies who did embark upon railway work did so as cheaply as possible, wasting no effort on marginal lines and planning routes with a minimum of tunnels, avoiding all obstacles requiring difficult engineering. When, a few years later, the state of Prussia did begin to actively encourage railway development, the motive was strategic rather than commercial. The authorities were conscious of the tense political situation and delicate balance of power and influence within the rest of Europe, and saw clearly the advantage that would be gained in time of war by the possession of a strong railway network.

104

A landmark in railway history was reached in 1843, when the first rail link between two different nations was opened, the 'Herbensthal' railway joining Belgium and Germany. From then on German railway construction continued apace. German rails had reached the French border by 1852, and the Dutch frontier by 1856. Within another year, Basle on the Swiss border was a destination announced at Frankfurt station. The rails then reached east to Russia, the two countries being linked in 1860.

The Baden State Railway, opened in 1839, imported six Sharp engines from Britain, and the presence of these well built machines spurred the German engineers on to produce their own designs. Within a couple of years, three major German railway locomotive works had been established; Maffei at Munich for the Bavarian State Railway, Kessler in Karlsruhe, and Borsig in Berlin. When August Borsig established his locomotive shop he began by copying closely the American Norris engines which had been running on the Berlin–Potsdam line. He produced a 4-2-2 engine, which performed very well set against equivalent machines from Britain. However, this first Borsig locomotive was soon returned to the workshops to be converted into a 2-2-2, which was named *Bleuth* after Borsig's technical institute teacher.

Above: King Ludwig of Bavaria's railway from Nüremberg to Fürth, opened in 1835. The locomotive is Stephenson's *Adler* (*Eagle*), imported from England together with its driver. (*The Mansell Collection*)

105

Above: The first train on the newly opened Leipzig–Dresden–Berlin line in 1839, hauled by Johan Schubert's locomotive *Saxonia.* (*Mary Evans Picture Library*)

This engine, nicknamed 'Spinning Wheels', was the forerunner of much later German development, presenting a tough challenge to the spread of Crampton types and becoming typical on northern railways.

Meanwhile, the Baden State Railway was receiving the first of the new Stephenson 'long boilers'. These too were copied by German engineers, mainly by the Kessler Works. However, the German versions were not entirely free of the unsteady running experienced in Britain and France. On one occasion, a long boiler was derailed. One of the passengers was none other than the future German Kaiser, Friedrich of Prussia, who was unamused. Consequently the long boiler engine was forbidden by law in his country.

A year later, in 1852, the length of operational track in Germany had increased to 4800 kilometres (3000 miles), and railway mania had at last taken hold. The state railways in Württemberg had been running American Baldwin 4-4-0s, and some Norris engines too, for nearly seven years, when Ludwig Klein was appointed chief railway technician. The imported engines had not lasted well, and were performing badly, so he ordered 15 improved Norris types from the Kessler Works. All the locomotives on the Württemberg system were of this type for the next 25 years.

In the 1850s, in true regimental fashion, the Prussian government set out to examine the science of locomotive construction, and ordered a Crampton style engine from Robert Stephenson, and a further eight Cramptons, with as many variations as possible, from the Berlin shops. They then tested these against a Borsig 2-2-2 design. The Cramptons were admired for their smooth running, experience of the long boiler having left a deep impression on Prussian minds, but finally their reliability was questioned. The engines were used, but soon scrapped.

The Hanover State Railway however introduced a French version of the Crampton engine on its lines, and ordered another 38 from German shops, the largest number that any German line had acquired. Eventually over 130 Cramptons were used on German railways. The French 'Bourbonnais' six-coupled freight locomotives crept in on the southern railway networks, and soon Borsig was copying them in the production of the 0-6-0 Simplon type. Borsig supplied Simplons to the Prussian State Railway, on which they worked for 30 years. The 'Bourbonnais' was the last ready-built engine to be imported, although foreign ideas continued to influence locomotive design in Germany as the country raced ahead of other nations in its railway development.

The railways of Germany took on a new importance when in 1862 Otto von Bismarck became chief minister of Prussia. Bismarck's goal was the unification of Germany under the leadership of Prussia, and he realized that the railways could play an important part in this undertaking. In 1870, when the Prussians invaded France during the Franco-Prussian war, one of Bismarck's trump cards was his battalions of soldiers specially trained in all aspects of railway operation. These soldiers took over the railways in northern France, swiftly repaired any damage that had been incurred, and enabled Bismarck's army to sweep quickly to Paris.

As a result of the complicated political alliances within Germany, the Franco-Prussian war hastened the unification of the member states. With the proclamation of the German Empire in 1871 came a more unified railway system. However, individual states still retained some autonomy and there was still suspicion and disagreement. When, for instance, Prussia decided to nationalize her railways, a few small states were persuaded to follow suit and move towards an all-German railway

Above: This early Borsig engine, the *Breda*, built in 1875, was exported to Sweden where it was in regular service until the turn of the century. It can now be seen at the Tomteboda museum, Stockholm. (*Colourviews*)

Left: The last of Berlin's 'baby trains', a class of tiny locomotives with matching rolling stock used on suburban lines, running between Spandau and Botzow between the wars. (*The Mansell Collection*)

Below left: A Borsig 4-4-0, built in 1900 and displayed at the World Exhibition in Paris. This class of superheated locomotives went into service on the main Prussian passenger routes. (*Mary Evans Picture Library*)

Below: From a very early stage the Prussian railway system was built with military considerations very much in mind, and when the First World War broke out in 1914 the Germans made good use of their railways to speed up the movement of their troops. These soldiers, packed into a locomotive's tender, are part of a trainload being transferred from France to East Prussia in September 1914. The photograph is from the British *Illustrated War News.* (*Western Americana*)

system; but others, notably Bavaria, determined to prevent central control residing in Prussia, hung on tenaciously to control of their own systems.

The new order of railway management under Prussia's influence led to a military style of discipline, with great emphasis on efficiency and a ban on trade unions. When railwaymen were addressed by their superiors, they were ordered to stand to attention and salute.

Borsig continued to play around with his 'Spinning Wheels' design and made a 2-4-0 that was soon to be used all over Germany, and particularly on the Cologne lines. This express was called the *Flieger* (*Flyer*) and this class of engine was known as the Prussian Standard. It was with this engine that Prussia sought to standardize the whole of Germany's railways. The trouble with this plan was that, although every state saw the value of standardizing, agreement just could not be reached on whose standard to use. The plan was dropped, to be revived many years later.

The Prussians continued with this contentious engine, however, and it became known as the P3 series; 700 of these engines were manufactured. The Magdeberg region took the P3 design and modified it, to produce their own version, the S1, of which 260 are known to have been built. Once again, the railways of Germany were still happy to go their separate ways in locomotive design.

In 1880 August von Borries, superintendent at the Hanover division of the Prussian State Railway, introduced a compound system, the principle of which had been demonstrated to him by Anatole Mallet three years earlier when he had visited Mallet's workshop. Borries converted some 2-2-0 tank engines working the branch lines into Germany's first two-cylinder compound engines. The Prussian 0-6-0s were from then on manufactured as two-cylinder compounds, and within a decade Prussia was using over 790 of them. The Prussian railways also toyed with de Glehn's 4-4-0 compounds, but it was the Baden state

Above: A turntable on the Deutsche Bundesbahn. One feature of steam locomotives was that before they could return up the line they would have to be turned round to face forward, whereas diesels had a driving cab at each end. (*M. Mehltretter, ZEFA*)

system that enthusiastically adapted their locomotives to the de Glehn style, demonstrating once again that they were the most open of all the German lines to new ideas.

Prussia took great exception to foreign companies like the Wagons-Lits making a profit from Germany's railway stock, so it introduced the *Duch Gangswagen* (D Trains). These were first class, vestibuled trains with connecting corridors between coaches. However, the D Trains presented very little competition to Wagons-Lits outside Prussia.

Although Prussia had been unable to enforce a centralized railway policy, state railways did co-operate to further the economic interests of Germany. Prussia introduced a variety of cheap goods rates, for instance, to enable the shipyards on the Rhine to obtain raw materials from distant sources as cheaply as possible. The economic motivation had replaced, for a while, the strategic considerations of railways, and profit margins had crept up to 40 per cent by the turn of the century.

Also at the turn of the century, an important German invention arrived which influenced the design of large locomotives all over the world. Wilhelm Schmidt of the Kessler locomotive works developed the notion of superheating, a method of reheating steam and increasing its pressure, applied after the steam has left the boiler but before it reaches the cylinders. This system, with its double advantage of increasing efficiency and lowering fuel consumption, was greeted with excitement

all over Europe. Existing engines were converted, and new engine designs were changed to accommodate the new method of achieving a powerful head of steam.

This was Germany's major technical contribution to the steam railway era. Unfortunately for the lovers of the steam locomotive, Germany also contributed to its downfall. It was in 1897 that Dr Rudolf Diesel, a graduate of Munich Technical College, made his four-cycle diesel engine, which would within thirty years begin irrevocably squeezing out the steam engines of the world. Germany was not the first country to develop the potential of the diesel engine, because she lacked the oil, and it was to be America, with her own wells, that would exploit this new invention first.

In the early 1890s the first Atlantic class engines to be built in Germany rolled out from the Maffei shops in Munich and became designated the 2D class. The 4-4-2 Atlantic locomotive had within four years been moulded into the Pacific class, which went into service all over Europe and America. The *Rheingold* was the first Pacific to work the German express passenger routes. The Pacifics were designated the S3-6 class, a series of locomotives that would produce some mammoth engines in years to come. With the advent of the new Pacifics and Atlantics the average speeds on some German railways increased from 48 km/h (30 mph) to 87 km/h (54 mph).

Above: A pair of 4-6-2 Pacifics pull a passenger express out of Bamberg station on the Deutsche Bundesbahn. Steam locomotives are no longer used in West Germany. (*M. Mehltretter, ZEFA*)

The lesson that trains could move armies across large distances in a fairly short time had been well absorbed during the Franco-Prussian war. In the intervening years strategic considerations had influenced much of the route planning for Germany's railways. The special railway battalions of soldiers, who could build and operate railways and, if necessary, destroy them efficiently, were inside proof of the military value Germany placed on railways. During the years leading up to the First World War many rail routes were established between France and Germany. Other new routes linked Germany with Belgium and Luxembourg. A line built by the Germans in 1913 connected the Liège railway with a short cut to Malmedy and was used by them in their invasion 10 months later. When war broke out, Belgium destroyed many of her own railways to thwart the enemy's advance.

After the defeat of Germany the map of Europe was once again redrawn. With the loss of some of her territory Germany's railways were greatly reduced. The Allies in Europe demanded 5000 locomotives as part of their war reparations. By 1920 Germany had completely nationalized her railways under the Deutsche Reichsbahn (DR), but in 1924 the Allies forced a return to a mixed system of public and private ownership under the Dawes plan to get Germany financially back on her feet.

The main problem that the DR faced was how to create a cohesive service out of the 210 different types of locomotives, many of them badly serviced, which were running in Germany. Therefore in 1925 a new standard steam locomotive was inaugurated, using a Pacific class engine that could still be seen running in East Germany in the mid-1970s. The old Bavarian locomotive works still continued to develop the pre-war S3-6 series. An example of this locomotive was introduced in Saxony and was known as the *Sachsenstoltz* (*Pride of Saxony*).

As the economic climate of Germany began to improve, so the railways' development became more adventurous, and in the early 1930s the DR began experimenting with streamlining. They wanted to discover whether the benefits of reduced wind resistance would be outweighed by heating problems and lack of draught for the fire. These fears proved groundless and the designs went ahead. Two 4-6-4 three-cylinder compounds were built by Adolf Wolff of the electrical firm AEG's Borsig works, and were delivered in 1935, the same year that Germany's railways celebrated their centenary at Nüremberg. These new streamlined trains achieved a speed of 200 km/h (124 mph). A year later the designs were changed, producing a 4-8-4 engine, employing certain modifications which André Chapelon was using in France at that time. These 'superlocos' would have been refined much more, had the process not once again been violently interrupted by another war.

During World War II Germany faced acute shortages of raw materials. At first this was met in the locomotive shops by stripping down old engines and substituting materials and parts wherever possible. Clearly this was only a short-term measure. The weird and ugly-looking machines that were hatched by this process during the early months of the war were known as *Ubergangskreigslokomotiven* – 'wartime transitional locomotives'. These engines coped for a short time, but by 1941 the demand created by an ever-expanding war front across Europe and North Africa could not be met by this engine and work began on a new standard war locomotive employing the minimum of

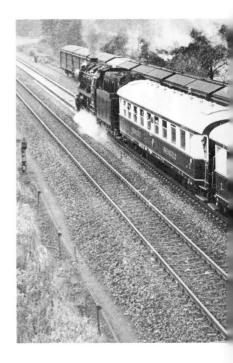

Above: The *Rheingold*, Germany's luxury international express train, pictured here in its final steam-powered form. The *Rheingold* travels from Holland and north-west Germany to Switzerland and Italy. (*John Titlow*)

Right: The streamlined Henschel-Wegmann locomotive on display to the world's press in Hamburg shortly after breaking the world speed record for a steam train in 1936, when it reached a speed of 199.7 km/h (124.1 mph). Much research on experimental high-speed steam locomotives was carried out in Germany in the 1930s. (*The Mansell Collection*)

Above: Some steam engines are still running in East Germany, including this fine example, a 4-6-2 Pacific photographed in 1977 at East Berlin before departing for Dresden. (*John Titlow*)

materials and labour. This design needed to be easy to operate and yet still meet a satisfactory standard of performance.

The result was the massive 2-10-0 designated the BR52 class. As the war raged on, 6400 BR52s were constructed and put to work supplying the armies and factories with reliable transportation. Working at full efficiency this engine could haul 1200 tonnes at a constant 65 km/h (40 mph). As fuel became in short supply, however, coke and briquettes were added to the coal, requiring two firemen to feed the fires constantly, and the standard of the engine's performance deteriorated. Few of these engines survived to 1945, when once again peace was established in Europe.

At the end of the war, German industry and communications were smashed; the long slow process of rebuilding began again. As after the First World War, Germany lost large areas of territory under the peace terms, and with them a good deal of railway. The country was split first into four, then into two. The two new German republics, West and East, each set up their own railway authorities: the Deutsche Bundesbahn (DB) in the West, the Deutsche Reichsbahn (DR) in the East. The East

113

Above: Two class 52 *Kriegsloks* (wartime locomotives) in service on East Germany's Deutsche Reichsbahn in 1972, at Stendal sheds. (*Brian Stephenson*)

Opposite above: This 2-8-0 heavy goods locomotive is assisted by a diesel engine (almost hidden at the back of the train) up one of the steep gradients of southern Germany. (*M. Mehltretter, ZEFA*)

Opposite below: A splendid class 02 Pacific, the first standard German locomotive, on the Deutsche Reichsbahn in 1977. Although no longer in regular service, it is still used on enthusiasts' trains. (*John Titlow*)

was undoubtedly the poorer of the two, and this was seen in its continued use of steam traction. West Germany on the other hand underwent the so called 'economic miracle', and through injections of foreign aid its railways quickly received the new diesel and electric locomotives which were swiftly taking over the railways of all the more advanced countries. The last steam locomotive to be built in West Germany was the very elegant Standard Series 10, a 2-6-2 express, which operated from Frankfurt. Only two of these locomotives were built, in 1957, and within a decade they were scrapped.

Bismarck's dream of a united Germany with a dominant role in Europe exercised a tremendous influence on the development of the German railway system; no other country's railways were planned with military considerations so much to the forefront. Five times the steam locomotives carried the German armies to war, only for the dream to end in a nightmare of destruction and defeat. When Germany rose from the ashes, the railway engines that contributed to that resurrection were diesel or electric ones. Apart from a handful of steam locomotives still working the lines in the East, the steam age in Germany ended with the scrapping of the two Series 10's in 1967.

The rest of Europe

The Austro-Hungarian Empire

At the beginning of the railway age, this remnant of the ancient Holy Roman Empire, ruled by the Habsburg dynasty, encompassed the territory of present-day Austria, Hungary, Romania and Czechoslovakia as well as large slices of Poland, Yugoslavia and Italy. The Empire's first steam railway was the Vienna–Brno line, the first section of which was opened in 1837, built by Count Carl von Ghega on behalf of the French banking family of Rothschild. The Rothschilds owned many lines across Europe and were building their own railway empire.

The line was diplomatically named Kaiser-Ferdinands Nordbahn, after the Emperor. It was operated by two Planet type engines named *Austria* and *Moravia*. Later the line introduced American Norris type engines, after its chief engineer visited America, where he saw the *George Washington* and became convinced that the running problems of the two countries were similar enough for the Norris engines to serve the line well. Soon these engines were in use all over Austria.

The engine was so attractive to the railways because it was of a simple construction, and could be reliably built in Austrian locomotive shops. This was an important consideration as the Empire was far less advanced in its industrialization than the other Great Powers, with the possible exception of Russia. However, the domestic construction of Norris types and other similar engines expanded so successfully that when Norris himself set up a locomotive works in Vienna to supply the Empire's needs, local competition put it out of business.

One of the most successful local locomotive builders was in fact a Scot, John Haswell, who had been seconded to Vienna by W. Fairburn & Co. of Manchester. Fairburn's supplied Haswell to the Vienna–Gloggnitz Railway along with the machine tools for its new locomotive shops. His first engine was a 4-4-0 called the *Wien*. It performed so well on the inclines of the Murzzuschlag–Laibach stretch of the line that the company was encouraged to build the next section which ran on to Gloggnitz. This very difficult line, which included a tortuous stretch over the Semmering pass, later became known as the Semmering line.

One of the early dreams of the railway pioneers in Austria was to connect the capital, Vienna, with the port of Trieste and the Habsburg possessions in northern Lombardy, now part of northern Italy. This offered tremendous strategic and economic advantages, but it meant going over the Alps. The building of the Semmering line was the most dramatic aspect of Austria's railway history. Who better to complete this arduous task, which George Stephenson had described as impossible, than Count von Ghega? Opponents tried to ruin von Ghega with libellous gossip about his alleged wasteful spending of government money, but without success.

Above right: A 4-4-0 series 4 standard locomotive of the Austrian State Railways. Built in 1884, this was the forerunner of a series of 4-4-0 models which were used extensively throughout the Austrian Empire. (La Vie du Rail *archives*)

Right: This massive 2-12-0 locomotive, designed by Karl Gölsdorf in 1911, was one of a series of large freight engines which would have helped shape the future of steam locomotives for many years to come had not the First World War disrupted development. (La Vie du Rail *archives*)

2-B Personenzuglokomotive
der Oesterr. Staats-Eisenbahn.
Erbaut von den Staatsbahnwerken Wien im Jahre 1884

Above. A class 93 tank
locomotive, built at the
Maffei works in Germany.
This engine was used mainly
for heavy work over short
distances. (*P. B.
Whitehouse/Colourviews*)

The work began in 1846, continued at a furious pace and was completed in 8 years. Hundreds lost their lives on the project from landslides, avalanches and the plague, which swept the construction sites killing 700 men. When the line was officially opened many foreign dignitaries were invited to the ceremony. Among them was Bismarck, still at that time a relatively minor figure, who narrowly avoided death when a plank spanning a 14 metre (45 ft) crevice collapsed. He only just managed to scramble to safety with the aid of some helpers. Had he failed to do so, it is difficult to avoid speculating as to how different the fate of Europe, not to mention the story of German railways, might have been.

Meanwhile the task of cutting a line through the Alps to Trieste was only half the battle. It still remained to find a locomotive capable of tackling the line. At the suggestion of a German railway magazine, the

Austrian authorities announced a competition to find the best engines for the Semmering line, offering a first prize of 20 000 Imperial ducats, with runner-up prizes. The conditions of the contest were necessarily tough, defining precisely the engine's axle weights, attainable speeds and the loads it was expected to haul. There was also, not surprisingly, an emphasis on downhill braking.

On the day of the contest in 1851 four engines arrived. The *Bavaria*, built by Joseph Maffei of Munich, was chain driven, so that the front axles and the tender's axles were all linked to the drive wheels, thus spreading the adhesion weight as much as possible. The *Weiner Neustadt*, built by the Austrian Neustadt shops, had two four-wheeled frames joined by a central pivot. This idea had already been patented by Meyer in France a decade before. John Cockerill of the Seraing locomotive works in Belgium entered the *Seraing*, which also had the double 'floating' wheel frames, but had the common firebox situated in the middle, making the engine symmetrical. This style later developed to become the Pacific articulated locomotive. The *Vindabona*, entered by John Haswell, was an 0-4-0 with two grates, two fire doors and common boiler housing.

Joseph Maffei's *Bavaria* took away the first prize, pulling the heaviest load most quickly while using the least amount of fuel. The *Seraing* was the only locomotive to complete all 20 scheduled runs under the rules of the contest. However, its fuel consumption was very high and it fell into third place behind *Wiener Neustadt* which, although proving unable to carry enough fuel and water, performed better under the rules of the competition. Haswell's entry failed miserably, threatening to tear up the track. The fuel stores of the *Weiner Neustadt* were enlarged, and together with the *Bavaria* it was

Above: This odd-looking little engine works on a mountain line, climbing the Schneeberg mountain in Lower Austria. In order to obtain sufficient grip on the steep track it uses Blenkinsop's old 'rack' principle. (*Spectrum*)

Above: A class 131 locomotive, first produced in 1905, one of many types of locomotive designed by the Austrian engineer Karl Gölsdorf. (La Vie du Rail *archives*)

sold to the State Railway, which successfully operated them on the Semmering line. The chain-drive mechanism of the *Bavaria* was later replaced with a complex linkage system.

The building of the Semmering line was the first time the state had financed railway construction, and the project left its finances exhausted. It withdrew from the railway scene, leaving the Rothschild and Pereire families, who had already built most of Austria's railways, to fight it out.

The external influence reached locomotive design too. Joseph Hall, an English engineer, had worked for the Maffei works in Munich, but moved to Austria where he spent two years at the Vienna locomotive shops. His influence was felt there for the remainder of the century, and his six-coupled locomotive became the most widely used in Austria, over 200 going into service on the Sudbahn alone. Two of these engines were still in use in 1965.

In 1846 the first Hungarian railway ran the 34 kilometres (21 miles) from Budapest to Vác. Two years later Hungary was thrown into turmoil by a revolution, which proclaimed the abolition of the monarchy and the establishment of a republic under the leadership of Louis Kossuth. The Austrians soon crushed the republic with the aid of Russia and reinstated the old king. However, in the same year Austria itself suffered serious internal disorder. The railways were taken over by the Austrian state during all this upheaval, but after the building of the Semmering line, they reverted to private ownership. When the Pereires took control of them and formed the Austrian State Railway Company, the Hungarian lines were also thrown into the deal.

The development of the Hungarian system mostly mirrored what was happening in Austria, with the exception of some locomotive work. One Hungarian invention was the Brotan boiler, used on tank engines, which was specifically designed to cope with the impure silty water found in the country.

In 1893 Karl Gölsdorf set about applying the compound engine as developed by Mallet and de Glehn to the Austrian situation. This was basically a question of altering the basic 4-4-0 two-cylinder compound engine to run successfully on the very light Austrian track. He had considerable success in this, and soon his 4-4-0s were used all over the Empire's system. Gölsdorf went on to build 2-8-0 two-cylinder compounds, which were the forerunner of the 'Mountain' locomotive, and of the modern freight locomotive. The engine was designated the 170 class in Austria, and could haul 550 tonnes up quite steep inclines at 26 km/h (16 mph). By the First World War 800 had been built. Gölsdorf also converted the Pacific design, by changing it into an 'Adriatic' 2-6-4, effectively a reverse of the Pacific. He also made much larger engines with ten- and twelve-coupled driving wheels.

As in much of Europe, Austrian locomotives stopped developing during the First World War. In 1917 the Empire was dismantled, and as a result many of its important railway lines lost their meaning. A railway system built to serve an Empire was simply inappropriate for a number of small ravaged states. However, moves had already been made before the war towards the nationalization of the railways, and in 1924 the process was more or less completed with the acquisition by the state of Sudbahn, the last of the big private railway companies. In the same year control of the railways passed into the hands of the newly created Federal Austrian Railways (OBB).

There was very little development of steam engines in Austria between the wars. When Hitler annexed Austria in 1939 the OBB was incorporated into the Deutsche Reichsbahn, and domestic control of the railways did not return until 1947. All the main lines were subsequently converted to diesel and electric trains. Some private lines remained, however, including the Graz–Koflach railway, which to this day uses steam locomotives for carrying coal.

Italy

Steam engines are still in use on some minor lines in Italy, despite the fact that the country adopted a policy of electrification at a very early stage. The first electric tram ran in Florence in 1890, and it could be said that the days of Italian main line steam railways were numbered almost from the outset.

At the beginning of the railway age, the Italian peninsular was divided between several different states, many of which were ruled by non-Italians. Each state had its own political and economic reasons for entering the railway speculation game. The first line, opened by the King of Naples in 1839, ran the five miles from Naples to Portici; or rather, to be more precise, from the royal residence at the foot of mount Vesuvius to the barracks and royal arsenal in Portici. This bold, militarily motivated plan was executed with some trepidation. The king had doubts about this new 'iron horse' and refused to travel on the first train, ordering a group of government employees and soldiers to go

Overleaf left: An ÖBB (ex-German) class 52 *Kriegslok* in service at Hieflau in 1969. (*Brian Stephenson*)

Overleaf right: The rail bridge link across the lagoon to Venice, linking the ancient city with Milan and the Italian rail network. The bridge took six years to build and was opened in 1846. (*Mary Evans Picture Library*)

instead. It was not until the experimental passengers had made the return journey to Portici that he would allow himself to be transported.

In northern Italy, the Austro-Hungarian Empire still controlled the plain of Lombardy, and under its auspices a line was built in 1840 from Milan to Monza. Later another line was added from Milan to Venice. In 1846 an important railway bridge was opened from the port of Mestri across the lagoon to Venice.

Pope Pius IX was one of the first Italians to envisage a national network of railways. His influence led to the opening of the Rome–Frascati railway, which he encouraged in order to attract more pilgrims to Rome. The grateful Frascati Railway Company presented the Pope with a personal saloon car for his use when travelling by rail. Quite apart from this coach, the Frascati railway generally offered a unique style of passenger travel, with coaches that were festooned with religious regalia and decorations. Many of the stations on the railways of the Papal States have been compared with cathedrals, decorated as they are with caryatids, ornate coats-of-arms and apostolic insignia.

In 1859, war broke out between Austria and the Italian state of Piedmont, which, aided by the French, gained some notable victories. In the following two years the skill of the statesman Cavour and the dramatic exploits of Garibaldi succeeded in creating a single unified country free from foreign control, and in 1861 Victor Emmanuel II of Sardinia was crowned King of Italy. One of the first consequences of this was the establishment of four major railway companies to operate the Italian network. The government offered various compensatory schemes for the construction of new routes. Florence was connected to the Milan–Rome line in 1864 and three years later a line running from Verona via Bolzano cut through the Brenner pass to Austria, linking Italy with the railways of Europe at Innsbruck.

Italy had a relatively undistinguished history in terms of steam railway engineering. The main exception to this was Cesare Frescot, who between 1889 and 1895 designed the powerful *Giovanna d'Arco* as well as the first European 4-6-0 with a separate tender, the *Vittorio Emmanuel II*. Another engineer named Plancher, of the Adriatico Railway Company, developed a four-cylinder compound engine, independently of de Glehn or von Borries, for the difficult Milan–Rome line. The route travelled through the Apennines, a demanding mountain range that needed a special locomotive to tackle it. Plancher designed the locomotive with the driver's cab at the front.

The topography of Italy, with its great Alpine sweep across the north and the Apennines down the centre, presented many problems for railway construction. In fact, more than five per cent of Italian railways are buried in 1800 tunnels. Until 1890 most of Italy's locomotives were imported; and it was to Austria, with her similar natural conditions, that the Italian railways went for ideas. Italy's most successful mountain locomotive was the 0-8-0 built by Neustadt of the Austrian railways, of which 106 were built, ten of which survived into the 1950s.

Apart from mountain passenger travel the other great headache facing Italian railways was how to move freight in and out of the major port of Genoa, surrounded by hills with a 1:30 incline. New locomotives were designed for this purpose. Unfortunately, all proved less than perfect, and most were removed to flatter areas of the Italian network. They were slowly replaced by electric engines.

Punctuality, never Italian railways' strongest point, was further hampered by the smoke and steam which clogged the many tunnels on the lines, severely restricting the number of trains allowed to pass through in any given hour. Clearly, the new electric engines could

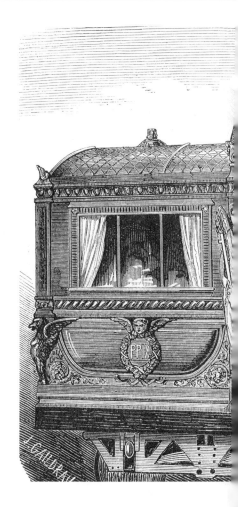

Above: The special saloon coach presented to Pope Pius IX in 1858 by the Frascati railway company. Less ornate versions of this saloon car dominated the style of Italian rail travel for half a century. (*Mary Evans Picture Library*)

Left: A nineteenth-century photograph of a local train, headed by a tank engine, waiting at Moncenisio station on the Italian side of the Fréjus tunnel linking France and Italy. Notice the wonderfully elaborate uniforms on the railway officials in front of the freight wagons. (*The Mansell Collection*)

Above: Two 2-6-0 tank engines 'doubled-up' for a heavy load. These engines can still be seen on some mountainous branch lines and industrial sites in Italy. (*J. M. Jarvis, ZEFA*)

solve these problems and from 1901 they began to be introduced in northern Italy.

After years of losing money, Italy nationalized her railways in 1905, and electrification continued apace. By 1939, although many steam locomotives had been received, mainly from Austria, in war reparations after the First World War, electrification had progressed to the extent that Italy was the leading country in the world in this new form of railway traction.

Scandinavia

Despite the tradition of economic co-operation between the four nations of Scandinavia, Denmark, Norway, Sweden and Finland advanced their railways in quite different ways. Denmark, for instance, had to face the problem that her territory was spread across numerous islands and stretches of water. Nevertheless, Denmark enjoyed some easy terrain on which to build her new railways. In one such area, Schleswig-Holstein, a railway was opened in 1844 running from Altona to Neumünster and on to Kiel, a distance of 145 kilometres (90 miles). Unfortunately, when this area was annexed by Prussia 20 years later, the line was lost.

Meanwhile another line had been opened in Copenhagen connecting the capital with Roskilde 30 kilometres (19 miles) away. Both these lines had been privately sponsored; the first state line was opened in 1862

Above: An impressive 2-6-0 passenger locomotive at Aosta in the Italian Alps, at the junction of the Great and Little St Bernard Passes. (*J. M. Jarvis, ZEFA*)

joining the north-eastern port of Aarhus with Randers. More lines quickly opened, and all were taken over by the Danish State Railways (DSB) in 1885.

Norway had much stiffer problems, with jagged mountains towering over small isolated coastal plains. Norway's rugged landscape provided countless problems for the railway designer, especially as many important population centres had grown up at the head of water inlets and fjords virtually cut off from the interior. Apart from this massive obstacle, Norway's railways were always modest as there was little industry or concentrated population to justify the cost.

The country's first railway ran from Oslo 69 kilometres (43 miles) north to Eidsvoll, the first section of a proposed route to Trondheim in the north-east. Although this first section opened in 1854, it was not until 1921 that the final destination was reached. The early Norwegian railways were firmly under the influence of the British, this first line being built by George Stephenson. Even the company rule book was written in English as well as Norwegian.

In Sweden a greater variety of terrain confronted the planners who met to advise the Swedish parliament on the construction of a national railway network. The southern plains of Scania presented only a few large lakes to hinder the progress of construction but the northern mountains stretching up into the Arctic Circle were a different matter. Like Norway, northern Sweden was no easy path for the railway planners, nor did it have a sufficiently large population to justify enormous expenditure on railways. However, the interior of northern Sweden held valuable mineral wealth which more than paid for the lines all over the country. Sweden also had much to gain from the use of railways for freight traffic, especially in winter when the Baltic froze over and became impassable.

In 1853 the Swedish parliament decided that the main railway routes would be state-owned from the outset, under the control of the Swedish State Railway (SJ). However the first steam railway, opened in 1856, was a private line connecting Nora to Ervalla, a distance of 18 kilometres (11 miles). The first state line ran from Malmö in the south to the important port of Gothenburg. This line together with the Malmö–Lund railway formed part of a system joining Gothenburg to Stockholm, the capital, on the east coast. Stockholm was not reached by rail until 1862, as part of a railway 'boom' lasting 20 years during which 5000 kilometres (3000 miles) of track were laid. Nearly all of these lines were in the south where it was relatively flat.

The Lapland Railway, which was built in 1902 to exploit the rich iron ore deposits around Kiruna, runs from within the Arctic Circle to the Gulf of Bothnia on the Baltic. An extension also runs west into Norway to the port of Narvik, which was little more than a fishing village until the railway came.

Finland was the last of the four Scandinavian countries to join the railway age. Until 1918 the country was part of the Russian Empire, so that when its first line opened in 1862, from the capital Helsinki to Hämeenlinna, the 108 kilometre (67 mile) route was laid to the standard Russian gauge of 5 ft (1.52 metres). All subsequent railways in Finland have kept this gauge. Finland, however, has had her own distinctive home-produced locomotives and railway equipment since 1874. Her last steam locomotives were taken out of service in 1975.

At the end of the nineteenth century there was an attempt to replace the strong German influence on Danish railways with a more indigenous style. The DSB appointed Otto Busse to design a new range of locomotives. His ideas were considered rather old-fashioned, but his version of the Atlantic outlasted all other European versions.

After the initial British influence had waned in Norway, much of her railway equipment was supplied by Sweden. Eventually Oslo was connected to Bergen, Stavangar and Trondheim, this line being served mainly by Norway's most notable contribution to locomotive design, the 2-8-4 four-cylinder compound express passenger engine. Although electrification began in Norway in 1911, steam ruled the rails until 1945.

From quite early in her railway history Sweden had a strong domestic

Above: A 2-4-0 locomotive, no. 9, built at the Canada works in Birkenhead, England, in 1865, and shipped to Denmark, pictured with the Danish royal coach in 1868. (*DSB Jernbanemuseet, Copenhagen*)

Left: Norway's most notable home-produced steam locomotive, the 2-8-4 4-cylinder compound engine known as the 'Dovregubben', was introduced in the 1930s on the newly-opened direct line from Oslo to Trondheim via Dovre. (*Norwegian National Railway Museum*)

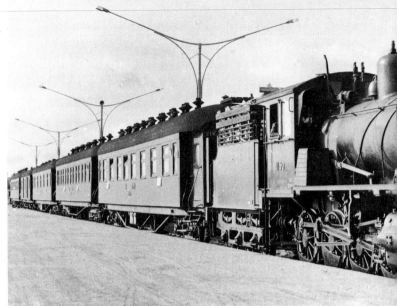

Left: An ex-Swedish State Railway 2-6-4T on the turntable at Wansford, on the Nene Valley Railway, England, where it is now preserved. Notice the snow ploughs on its front, essential pieces of equipment in the Scandinavian winter. (*Spectrum*)

Above: A passenger train, hauled by a woodburning 2-8-0 locomotive, waiting at Rouaniami, Finland. (*P. B. Whitehouse/Colourviews*)

Below: A tank engine in Portugal, hauling mixed traffic up through the hills north of Vidago on the narrow gauge Corgo railway. (*J. M. Jarvis, ZEFA*)

locomotive manufacturing industry, with a high level of exports. Electrification began quite early, using the readily available sources of hydro-electric power. The first line to be converted was a section of the Stockholm–Roslagen railway in 1894. By the end of the Second World War Sweden was second only to Italy in her electrification progress. Between the wars, the Ljungstrom brothers, chief engineers at the works of the Nydquist and Holm Company built one of the most successful steam turbines in the world, but it arrived too late to combat the growing inroads made by electric and diesel power.

Spain and Portugal

The first Spanish railway was built thousands of miles from home, in the Spanish colony of Cuba. Built in 1837, it ran from Havana to Los Guines. It was another 11 years before the first line opened on the Spanish mainland, connecting Barcelona and Mataro. From about 1856 there was heavy investment in Spanish railways from French business interests, and this accelerated the construction of new track.

Portugal, not wanting to be left out of the picture or remain cut off from an interconnecting Europe, began building her own system. The first line opened in 1856, running from Lisbon to Corregado, but its first run did not augur well for Portuguese railways. The inaugural train bearing the King and various important dignitaries broke down, and the royal party had to disembark and make their own way back. The Portuguese adopted the same track gauge as Spain, but although one could travel from Lisbon through Spain to the rest of Europe by the early 1870s, the lack of continuity of gauge with France hindered trade

Right: The ultimate Spanish locomotive, the Chapelon-type 2-10-2 compound, on the Arcos Bank in 1967. This engine could haul 2600 tonnes at 53 km/h (33 mph). (*J. M. Jarvis, ZEFA*)

Below right: A 2-6-2 Spanish tank engine taking on water on the narrow gauge Alcoy Gandia railway in 1963. (*J. M. Jarvis, ZEFA*)

in the Iberian peninsula, particularly in Portugal. The situation was not eased until the early 1900s, when Spanish workshops developed variable gauge rolling stock to obtain international compatibility.

The whole peninsula presented very rough terrain for the steam locomotive. Mountainous in some areas, flat in others, it made such a variety of demands that for a long time some routes had to be chopped into sections worked by different specialized locomotives. Locomotives in the peninsula were heavily influenced by French locomotive design, and French engineers worked hard at solving this problem. They had some success, notably with the *Mammoth*, a Polonceau type six-coupled (0-6-0) long boiler.

The turn of the century saw Madrid connected to all important centres on the peninsula, with locomotive design influenced more and more by Austria and southern Germany, although the Spanish were by now building their own engines, and making many design improvements. During the First World War the idea was hatched to build a railway tunnel under the Straits of Gibraltar, a project which was greeted with instant enthusiasm by France, which saw the advantages it offered in giving her closer contact with her colonies in north Africa. The shortest distance between the two 'pillars of Hercules' is only 16 kilometres (10 miles). Unfortunately, however, the sea bed on this route reaches a depth of 550 metres (1800 ft), so a slight detour was needed, bringing the total distance between each mouth of the proposed tunnel to 31 kilometres (19 miles). An engineer named Jevenios was put in charge of the project, his brief being to design every aspect of the railway that was to run from Tarifa under the Straits to Morocco. Year after year, however, the project was delayed and starved of sufficient funds, until it was finally abandoned with the onset of the Spanish Civil War.

In 1943 the Spanish railways were nationalized by General Franco, bringing them under the control of the Spanish National Railways (RENFE). Steam engines continued to be used until the 1960s when they were phased out and replaced by diesels.

The Benelux Countries

From the start, Belgium and the Netherlands had very different approaches to railways, and their enthusiasm for the new invention differed correspondingly. In Belgium the start of the railway age coincided with the gaining of independence from Habsburg rule in 1831, and the newly formed Belgian government set out immediately to assert its political strength through the building of railways. Another attraction was that railways enabled the Belgians to offer genuine competition to the ports and waterways of the neighbouring Netherlands.

Belgium's first line, joining Brussels to Malines, was opened in 1835, the opening being attended by George Stephenson, who was technical consultant. The royal family were also present, publicly displaying their support for the new steam railway. Within 5 years two more lines were opened. One ran from Antwerp in the north through Brussels southwards to France. The other ran from the western port of Ostend to Louvain and on into Germany. The two routes crossed at Malines, where the state railway built its first locomotive workshops.

Left: The opening of the Brussels–Malines railway in 1835. Great excitement surrounded the event as it marked the completion of Belgium's first major national project after the achievement of independence in 1831. (*Mary Evans Picture Library*)

Below: A rather whimsical print of 1847 depicting an early Dutch railway. Railways were greeted with less enthusiasm in Holland than in most other countries. (*The Mansell Collection*)

In the Netherlands railways met with little support, as most future investment was earmarked for the steam barges with which the Dutch were trying to attract international freight traffic on to the inland waterways in which Holland is so rich. The Dutch also saw little need for railways as the capital was already within two days' reach of even the furthest place in their small country. It took a personal guarantee from the king that dividends would unfailingly be paid on investments before railway construction began. The first line opened in 1839 from Amsterdam to Haarlem, powered by a Stephenson locomotive called the *Arendt.*

Very little Dutch expertise emerged to continue railway development, and so the railway companies imported engineers from Britain and France, who in turn ordered the necessary equipment from home. The Netherlands were badly deficient in heavy engineering capacity and it was the French Gouin Company that constructed its most notable

133

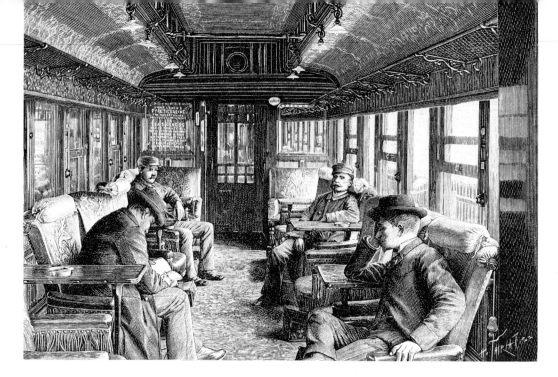

example of railway engineering, the rail bridge at Moerdijk. The bridge was 1040 metres (3412 ft) long and was financed mostly with British money. It forged an important link between Amsterdam and the German railway system at Cologne.

For some reason, which was never made clear, the Dutch stipulated a 2 metre ($6\frac{1}{2}$ ft) gauge for their rails, which meant that continuity of travel was impossible when the German frontier was reached at Emmerich. The scenes at Gloucester in England were mirrored as goods and people had to be transferred on to trains of the German gauge, and vice versa.

The lack of engineering expertise in the Netherlands was not reflected in Belgium. There engine works were set up, and many home-built locomotives were used on the state railway system. Although Belgium's locomotives did little to influence design world-wide, she did contribute the Walschaert valve gear, named after its inventor, in 1844. This was a complicated system of levers and connecting rods which controlled the direction of the engine and the amount of steam

Right: Construction
workers pose for a memorial
photograph at the Swiss end
of the Gotthard tunnel after
the tunnel's completion in
1882. (*The Mansell
Collection*)

available to the cylinders. Before Walschaert introduced this system
most locomotives had used Stephenson's valve gear, which lacked the
sophistication required for the ever developing steam locomotive. Soon
the Walschaert gear was adopted by most locomotive works.

Without doubt, however, Belgium's greatest contribution to railway
history was the Wagons-Lits, the luxury coach company established in
1876 by Georges Nagelmackers of Liège, who had seen and admired the
Pullman cars of American railways and set out to provide even greater
comfort for European rail passengers.

The First World War had a disastrous effect on the Belgian rail
system. A vast amount of railway stock was deliberately destroyed in
1914 to prevent the invading Germans from using it. After the war
financial restraints hindered the rebuilding programme. In 1926 Belgian
railways were nationalized under the SNCB (Société Nationale de
Chemins de Fer Belgiques), and the Netherlands followed suit 12 years
later. All the reconstruction and reorganization, however, was
shattered again by the next war, from which Belgium emerged with
only 144 locomotives left intact. After the war, as in other parts of
Europe, the steam locomotive no longer played a part in the reconstruction of the Benelux railways.

Switzerland

The first Swiss railway was opened in 1847, between Zurich and Baden.
The line, called the *Spanisch Brötli Bahn* ('Little Spanish Bread
Train') was run by two Norris 2-4-0s built at the Kessler works called
the *Rhein* and the *Reuss*. Soon the country was swamped with small
lines snaking round the foot of mountains and across valleys, despite

the lack of capital available. The task was obviously enormous and required many tunnels and viaducts. The first of these tunnels was cut for the Gotthard railway and opened in 1882. The most famous was the Simplon, built in 1906 and followed by the Lötschberg tunnel 7 years later which connected the Simplon with eastern France. When these great Alpine tunnels were built Switzerland became a crossroads through which passed much of Europe's freight traffic.

Much of Switzerland's railway hardware was imported from her neighbours, although her mountain locomotives were developed at home, notably Weyermann's 2-6-0 three-cylinder compound engine. Within 15 years 147 of these had entered domestic service.

Switzerland's lack of indigenous fossil fuels coupled with the abundance of hydro-electric power prompted an early decline in the steam locomotive. The first Swiss electric train entered service in 1893, and in fact many lines were electrified from the start before steam had fully made its mark on Swiss railway history. The Swiss were already damming their lakes for electricity when the steam locomotive was still cutting virgin territory on the other continents of the world.

In Europe, perhaps more than anywhere else, the railways became the melting pot of culture and trade. The steam locomotives speeding across the frontiers of Europe played an important part in confirming the industrialized culture that we have inherited, naming mobility and punctuality as watchwords of the age. Within each country of Europe railway construction finally established the centralized society. Moreover, when the map of Europe changed overnight, as it did more than once during the age of steam, the railways alone were left to testify to the frontiers of yesterday.

Britain rules the rails

India

In 1900 the British Empire comprised 18 million sq kilometres (11 million sq miles) of territory, or 20 per cent of the earth's surface, on which a quarter of the world's population lived. The first seeds of this Empire were sown in 1600, with the granting by Elizabeth I of a charter allowing the East India Company a monopoly of trade with the East Indies. So big did the Company become that soon its commercial interests and the political circumstances of the East Indies became inseparable. It achieved tremendous power in India, on the one hand by playing one local ruler off against another to secure commercial concessions for itself, and on the other by maintaining government favour through the loan of enormous sums of money. When railways began spreading across the globe, the East India Company quickly saw their commercial value in India and set about planning their construction.

In the early 1840s India was ripe for railways. For the vast subcontinent, with its numerous exportable commodities and huge potential markets for British goods, railways were a natural development of British rule. Nevertheless, it took a decade of discussion and legislation before any lines were built. The directors of the EIC resided in London, a formidable group of men who had the final say in all Indian commercial activities. They were still very powerful, but they were no longer as confident a colonizing force as they had been in the eighteenth century. The Company was facing increasing political pressure both in India and in Britain, and their charter which was coming up for renewal in 1853 was in danger of being rescinded.

Before the railways could be built two things had to be decided: which gauge to use for the track, and what financial guarantee to offer investors. The guarantees were promises made by the EIC to pay a dividend to the new railways companies' shareholders should they fail to make an operating profit. The EIC wanted to offer 3 per cent, whereas the railway companies, led by the East India Railway Company (formed in 1845) wanted a 5 per cent guarantee. Much of this argument was conducted in London, mostly by continual lobbying of Parliament figures. The East India Railway Company eventually extracted the 5 per cent guarantee. It was an expensive way to encourage railway speculation, but an effective one.

The question of gauge was less contentious. The EIRC preferred the standard British 4 ft 8½ in (1.43 metres), but was prepared to leave the matter to the Indian colonial administration. Lord Dalhousie, Governor-General of India based in Calcutta, suggested 6 ft (1.83 metres). Frederick Simms, his consultant engineer, suggested the compromise of 5 ft 6 in (1.68 metres), and this became the standard adopted. This broad gauge was favoured not for the development of wider

Above: On the narrow gauge Darjeeling–Himalaya railway in north-east India passengers are apt to hop on at any point and hold on to whatever comes to hand! (*Spectrum*)

locomotives, as Brunel argued in England, but to overcome the high, cyclonic winds which any Indian railway would have to face.

After much bureaucratic and political dithering, India finally got her first railways in 1853. In fact, the running of the first Indian locomotive was claimed by both the East Indian Railway, which had its first line from Howrah near Calcutta to Hooghly, and the Great Indian Peninsula Railway, running from Bombay to Thana. From the outset, the various railway companies aimed to construct lines of priority importance. The EIR's first aim was to provide a line to tap the coal resources of Raniganj, which it achieved by 1855, and then to proceed along the Ganges plain to Delhi, where it arrived in 1864. From Delhi, the EIR pushed on towards the sensitive north-west frontier. The GIPR set out to link the second great centre of trade, Bombay, with the Ganges, eventually linking with the EIR network. By 1870 it was possible to travel by rail direct from Bombay to Calcutta. A third company, the Madras Railway, pushed from Madras towards Bombay to link up with the GIPR. This line was completed in 1871.

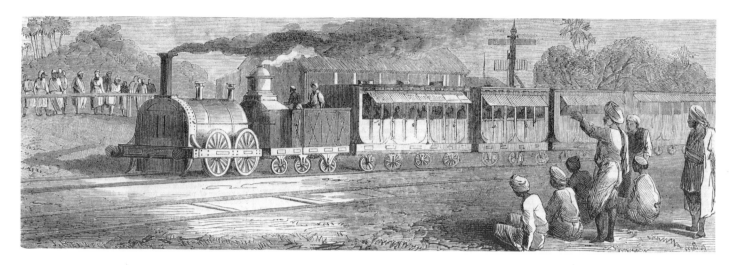

The guarantee system attracted vast quantities of capital, mostly from Britain, and by 1868 there were eight railway companies operating in India, with 6500 kilometres (4000 miles) of rail in use and a further 3200 kilometres (2000 miles) under construction. Despite the seemingly unlimited flow of capital, however, the railway construction industry was still underfed in terms of resources. Everything for the railways had to be imported, at enormous cost. The most expensive line to be built, the coastal route from Baroda to the Ganges owned by the Bombay, Baroda and Central India Railway, cost £20 000 per mile to lay. The consolations for the railway companies were that Indian labour was cheap, and the legal costs involved in 'right of way' disputes were low.

The East India Company finally lost its charter in 1858, and was replaced by a government of India under a viceroy. Immediately the government assumed responsibility for the guarantees taken on by the East India Company, and decided in all railway projects after 1868 to finance the construction itself. The government had already had to rescue the bankrupt Calcutta and South Eastern Railway, assuming ownership in 1862.

As government funds were not so freely available as those from private enterprise, the original intention to keep the broad gauge was reviewed. A new gauge, the metre width (3 ft 3 in) was decided upon, enabling railways to be built at half the cost of the broad gauge. It was felt that a narrow gauge was better than no railway at all. This was especially so in the areas of the Punjab and the Rajputana, where a railway would attract limited traffic but would have immense strategic importance. Therefore the first metre gauge line was opened from Rajputana to Malwa in 1879.

After 1880 it was decided once again to encourage private companies to be involved in initiating future lines, with the condition that the metre gauge should be reserved for branch lines, while the broad gauge would be standard for main lines. This condition was not always respected, however, in the face of the obvious economic advantages of the narrower gauge. The situation was aggravated by the construction of some 2 ft (0.61 metre) and some 2 ft 6 in (0.76 metre) lines, and the problem of differing gauges remains with Indian railways to this day.

In 1903 there were 41 740 kilometres (25 936 miles) of track, with 33 different administrations controlling the Indian railways. Five of these administrations were princely states. They varied from playthings for

Above: A train on the East Indian Railway, from an 1863 edition of *The Illustrated London News.* The following year the main line of the EIR, pushing outwards from Calcutta, arrived at Delhi. (*Mary Evans Picture Library*)

Right: This photograph was taken during the construction of the East Bengal Railway, 1869–72. The railways quickly became the largest single employer in India. (*India Office Library. Photo: A. C. Cooper*)

Below right: The Duke of Edinburgh boarding a train on the Great Indian Peninsular Railway at Parell in 1870, the year the railway linked up with the EIR, making it possible to travel direct from Bombay to Calcutta. (*Mary Evans Picture Library*)

rich potentates to large, important ventures providing a real benefit to the local population. Many of the private companies operating lines had their offices in London.

Various problems plagued the Indian railways after the First World War, and it was felt that the remote and unco-ordinated management system was at fault. From 1925 onwards, the government began to assume direct ownership and responsibility for the operation of the railways. A three-man Railway Board, responsible to the Viceroy, was formed to supervise matters. Commercially, the inter-war years were poor, with reduced freight and passenger travel and unreliable profitability. The railways became indispensable again with the outbreak of the Second World War.

In 1945, when the war ended, there were promises in the air for the independence of India. Within two years independence had been granted, but it did not immediately bring peace. The railways became the focus for fighting between Moslems and Hindus, in a wave of violence that culminated in Gandhi's assassination by a Hindu fanatic in 1948.

India's locomotives

From the beginning, most of the hardware for Indian railways was imported from Britain. The first locomotives used were 2-4-0s and 0-4-2s, plus some 2-2-2 tanks. These were later replaced by 4-4-0s for passenger duties and 0-6-0s for freight, very much reflecting developments in Britain. As freight traffic accounted for two-thirds of all revenue, the 0-6-0s were the most common in the early days. Of these the medium-gauge F series, built in Scotland, were the best known.

At the turn of the century the British Engineering Standards

Opposite: An Indian 4-4-2 broad gauge locomotive, built in 1907 by the North British locomotive company, and now preserved at Delhi. (*C. M. Gammell*)

Below right: British and Indian engineers on the scene of a train crash in about 1890. Few Indians obtained responsible positions on the railways before the First World War. (*The Mansell Collection*)

Below: A local train rounding Agony Point, a spectacular loop on the East Bengal Railway, in the 1890s. (*India Office Library. Photo: A. C. Cooper*)

Association began work on an Indian standard locomotive which would operate on the medium and broad gauge. The 0-6-0s were maintained, and were joined by 2-6-4Ts and improved 4-4-0s. In addition, the 2-8-0 was introduced, as well as the very successful 4-6-0, which continued to be built until 1951 and of which 70 were still in service in 1965.

In 1919 another locomotive committee was set up to decide on replacements for these BESA locomotives. They sent a list of their requirements to London, where designs were executed and the construction carried out. The designers followed the worldwide trend and supplied India with Pacifics for passenger work and Mikados for freight. Almost immediately these locomotives were found to be unsatisfactory, but not before 284 of them had been built. Some of them spent three out of every eight years in the repair shops, usually with problems in the main frames.

There was also a suspicion that these locomotives were responsible for a number of accidents, and after a particularly serious derailment at Patna in 1937 some lines withdrew their Pacifics and Mikados from service. A Pacific locomotive committee was set up to look into the matter. They reported in 1939, advising a host of improvements; but the war intervened. The failure of the Pacifics led to an unusual longevity for the Atlantics.

In 1940, Indian railways operated 5347 locomotives on the broad gauge lines, 2320 on the medium gauge, and 302 on the narrow gauge systems. During the war many engines were imported from America and Canada; 1000 standard wartime 2-8-2s went to the broad gauge lines and 300 'Mawd' 2-8-2s to the medium gauge. Nevertheless the postwar railways were short of locomotives, and the ones they had were in many cases past their prime.

The new replacements were improved Pacifics and Mikados, with

Above: A nineteenth-century photograph of a train crossing the Dapoorie viaduct, one of the countless works of engineering built during the construction of the Indian railway system. (*India Office Library. Photo: A. C. Cooper*)

Above left: Railway travel in India, from a picture book of the 1870s. (*Mary Evans Picture Library*)

alterations made on the basis of their previous experience in India. The 4-6-2 WP passenger class locomotive was introduced, and in 1947 this engine with some variants became the standard locomotive for India. These were the last steam engines built in India, or anywhere in the world, the last one being built in the Chittaranjan locomotive shops in 1972, by which time 1908 of this class of engine had been built, of which 2450 were still in operation in that year. In 1976 India still had 8000 steam locomotives working the lines, and steam traction is likely to persist in the country for many years to come.

Indian railways: recent history

One great benefit the railways brought to India was in the area of famine relief. Many of India's endemic famines were not caused by shortages of food as such but by bad distribution. There are many recorded examples of relief having been brought to an area just in time

Overleaf left: Flood damage on the East Indian Railway in 1943; the photograph shows the first train crossing a temporary bridge over the Damodar river in Bihar. The site of the original bridge, swept away by the swollen river, is marked by the broken rails in the foreground. (*India Office Library*. Photo: *A. C. Cooper*)

Overleaf right: A freight train steams through the palms on the Colombo–Kandy line in Sri Lanka. (*Enrico, ZEFA*)

145

because of the railways. The railways certainly did not solve all India's problems; but at times even the poorest Indian had cause to feel grateful to them.

There is no doubt that Indian railways have a character all their own. There is, for instance, none of the European preoccupation with speed. Only the crack mail trains on the run from Bombay to Calcutta ever made any attempt at speed, and even they averaged only 56 km/h (35 mph) in the 1920s. Less important services were slower, branch and feeder lines slower still, and freight trains between Calcutta and Lucknow averaged 6 km/h (4 mph). The conditions enjoyed (or suffered) by passengers were spartan. There were four classes: first, second, intermediate and third. There were of course very many more third class passengers than first class; in fact the ratio was about 150:1, and Indian passenger railways made most of their profits from their (usually) patient third class customers. This did not prevent railway staff from treating third class passengers contemptuously. One small example of this was that some first and second class carriages were marked 'Reserved for Ladies' while the equivalent third class carriages were marked 'Women Only'.

After independence attempts were made to soften this class distinction. First class was abolished in 1955, and the standard of comfort in the remaining classes substantially improved. In 1959, for instance, electric fans were installed in third class carriages.

Another improvement was the introduction of the *janata* (people's) trains, which were third-class-only expresses. In earlier days schedules had been arranged so that an uninterrupted third class long distance journey was almost impossible.

The Indian talent for bureaucracy and politicking has had a noticeable effect on the railways throughout their history. It must be remembered that the building of the country's first lines were delayed for almost ten years by such activity. Bureaucracy also saddled Indian railways with some very inefficient procedures. Running schedules tended to stay fixed for many years, because so many people would have to be consulted before a change could be made. Lines were often built

Above: The Lucknow express leaving Cawnpore station on the East Indian Railway in the 1930s. The station had been opened by the Viceroy in March 1931 amid much acclaim of its architectural splendour. (*The Mansell Collection*)

along particular routes more because of the pressure of a local politician than to fulfil a real demand.

As often happens in a bureaucratic structure, inefficiency extended into deliberate corruption. Quantities of freight goods might shrink alarmingly between source and destination; valuable reservations might be unobtainable until the appropriate official received a gratuity. It was estimated in 1972 that one-seventh of all the coal bought by Indian Railways was lost through pilferage.

Railways have often been the focus of violence in India. Under the British, the railways were the most visible and tangible representation of foreign rule, and were therefore an obvious target for nationalists, disgruntled sections of the community, or plain bandits.

One of the saddest episodes in the history of India, and of her railways, was the immediate post-independence violence between Hindus and Moslems. The decision to split the Empire into religious groupings led Moslems in India to flee to Pakistan, and Hindus in Pakistan to flee to India. The railways attempted to handle this traffic, and in August and September of 1947 the railways carried 700 000 refugees. Such trains were often attacked by religious activists of the opposite faith. In September a trainload of Moslems was attacked at Amritsar and 3000 passengers were murdered. A few days later a trainload of Hindu and Sikh refugees was ambushed near Lahore and 1500 died. Railway workers were among both the victims and the perpetrators of such atrocities.

Today the railways are still a target for local or national protest, which may or may not have anything to do with the railways themselves; although such protests are not of course comparable with the events of 1947.

As we enter the 1980s, the subcontinent of India has a vast railway

network beset by tremendous problems. But, as India attempts to join the ranks of the industrialized nations, railways are still playing a vital part in her progress. While enthusiasts in Europe and America nostalgically enjoy running steam locomotives on private lines, in India the steam engine is still being used as it was originally intended.

In many ways, railways and the Indian way of life will never really be compatible. Although the fabric of Indian society was to an extent re-shaped (though certainly not destroyed) by the railways, it was they that really had to be adapted to accommodate such a marriage. The railways certainly opened up the hinterland of the subcontinent and enabled easier exporting of its raw materials. Cotton was the best example, destined for the mills of Lancashire, and it was from this English textile county that a large proportion of capital came for the Indian railways. At the same time India was opened up to the importing of western goods, especially railway hardware. For example, in 1904 Britain exported to India £570 425 worth of steam locomotives, £744 649 worth of rails, and £141 529 worth of sleepers. These figures accounted for half the total British exports of railway hardware.

Western modernization was greatly resented on the subcontinent, and the railway was seen as the symbol of this modernization. The necessity for punctuality and precision was alien to the Indians. The railways tended to break down the caste barriers, indeed they intro-duced a new industrial caste. This industrial caste was very important to the country's development, and from the early days railways were the largest single employer. By 1870 90 per cent of the railway staff were Indians, but not a man amongst them held an office of any responsibility. Drivers and mechanics were Europeans, often dis-charged soldiers, who were not always of spotless character and who made little attempt to mix with the surrounding society, remaining in

Above: The Indian railway station has always since the arrival of railways been a meeting place and a colourful centre of local life, as this pre-war photograph of Allahabad station vividly shows. (*India Office Library. Photo: A. C. Cooper*)

149

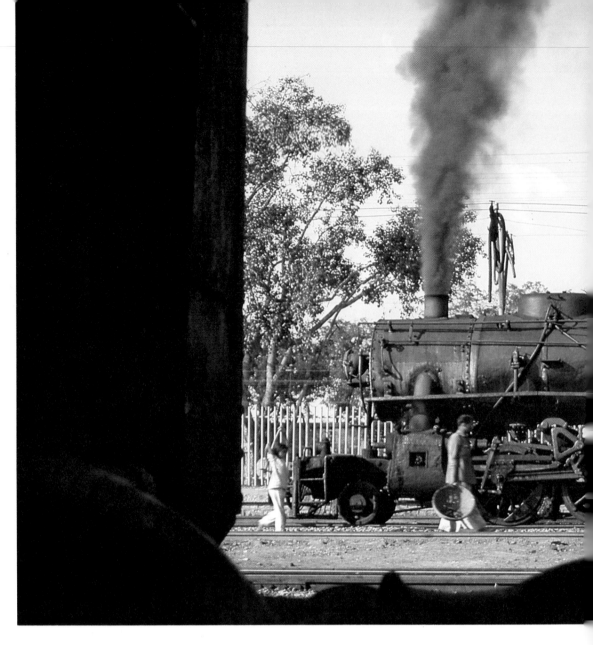

their own groups and often treating the Indians with contempt. The Europeans received double the wages of the Indians, much of which was usually spent on drink. For them it was a hard and not particularly pleasant life, made worse by their vulnerability to India's many endemic diseases. In fact 5 per cent were removed annually by death or disabling illness.

In 1890 all posts were theoretically thrown open to Indians, but the examinations were in English, giving a Briton of mediocre talents the advantage over the cleverest Indian. By 1910, out of 800 top positions, only 74 were occupied by Indians. Within a few years, however, as the population began to protest more loudly at its subservient position, a fairer recruitment system was introduced.

In May 1893 the young Gandhi was a passenger on the overnight sleeper from Durban to Pretoria in South Africa, where he was to represent some Indian businessmen in court proceedings in his capacity as a lawyer. In the middle of the night a white man entered his first class compartment and ordered Gandhi into the baggage car. Gandhi, holding a first class ticket, refused. At the next station, Maritzburg, the white man called the police, and they evicted Gandhi from the train. The train pulled away, leaving Gandhi alone and cold on the station platform. He spent the night awake, huddled from the cold in the waiting room, pondering on his first encounter with the brutality of racial

prejudice. When dawn finally broke on the little station, the timid withdrawn youth was a changed person. The little lawyer had reached the most important decision of his life: Mohandas Gandhi was going to say No! Much later, he forced the South African authorities to allow well-dressed Indians to travel first or second class on the railways. Later still, Gandhi led India to independence.

Africa

'The railway is my right hand, the telegraph my voice'
Cecil Rhodes

Although the 'dark continent' was littered with explorers, colonialists and missionaries in the nineteenth century, it was the empire builder Cecil Rhodes who made perhaps the greatest long term impact on it. Rhodes made his fortune by the discovery of diamonds at Kimberley, South Africa, and in order to get the maximum benefit from the mines commissioned a railway running from Cape Town to Kimberley in 1869. Rhodes had a great vision of gaining the whole of Africa for the British Empire, and regarded the proposed Cape-to-Cairo railway as essential to the fulfilment of his dream. However, when the railway penetrated the Transvaal it was to exploit the discovery of gold there, rather than

for any more lofty reason. The commercial interest in building railways was usually stronger and more quickly realized than any Imperial consideration.

With the establishment of Rhodesia in 1887 the railways began to spread north, searching out mineral wealth, and always striving towards the ultimate destination, Cairo. In 1897 the line reached the Zambezi river, with the great Victoria Falls in its path.

David Livingstone, the Scottish explorer and missionary, was in 1855 the first white man to see these magnificent falls, and his description had captured Rhodes' imagination to such an extent that he gave orders for the Zambezi to be spanned by a bridge built close enough to the falls for the spray to wet each passing train. The result was a spectacular piece of engineering. Initially a cableway, capable of holding 10 tonnes, was thrown across the gorge so that the bridge could be built from both sides simultaneously. The bridge was finally completed in 1905. Rhodes, who never saw the falls, which were over 2600 kilometres (1600 miles) from Cape Town, had died three years before.

Rhodes' dream of the Cape-to-Cairo railway was never realized. The line did, however, reach Kindu in the Congo (now Zaire). From there a gap of 1700 kilometres (1000 miles) still existed before the railways began again in the Sudan, and there was a further gap of 240 kilometres (150 miles) between Sudanese and Egyptian railways. 'Without a railway, your Majesty,' the explorer Stanley advised the King of Belgium, 'the Congo is not worth a penny.' King Leopold II heeded Stanley's advice, and during the 1890s the railway pushed into the Congo interior. The work was done by 2000 African labourers under the direction of European engineers and craftsmen. The conditions were unbearable for the Africans, who had been rounded up as forced labour. When they eventually refused to carry on, the authorities responded by importing 500 Chinese workers, who were renowned for their efforts on the Union

Above: Cecil Rhodes' dream come true: the bridge spanning the Victoria falls, now in Zambia. Sadly, Rhodes died before seeing his ambition fulfilled. (*C. M. Whitehouse/Colourviews*)

Pacific Railroad in America. Within a few weeks half had died or deserted. The railway pushed forward, however, and the first train finally rolled into Stanleyville on 16 March 1898.

Unlike in India, the British did not have exclusive control of the continent; many other colonizing forces were advancing through the interior by rail. The French had laid 120 kilometres (75 miles) of track between the villages of Kayes and Bafulabe in the western Sudan. Italian engineers were surveying a route over a jagged mountainous wrinkle from Massawa on the Red Sea to Asmara in Eritrea. The Belgians were constructing a railway joining the Atlantic port of Matadi with the navigable reaches of the lower Congo river. Portugal was operating a line in Angola, and constructing another in Mozambique. Germany was shortly to begin work on a track from Tanga to the interior of her East African territory. Britain did not want to be left behind, especially with the tremendous mineral resources of her territory in the south and west.

Even as late as the 1880s people in Britain saw Africa as a red herring. The wealth being exploited at Kimberley and the Transvaal was insignificant compared to the problems of occupation and development. Then suddenly Africa began to be an arena for subtle international

politics. The British Prime Minister, Lord Salisbury, was persuaded that the 1889 treaty signed between Italy and Abyssinia, granting Italy an Imperial claim to the banks of the Blue Nile river (a tributary of the Nile in the eastern Sudan) was a dangerous threat to India, the shining star of the British Empire. For complex reasons Uganda, where the Nile rose, suddenly leapt to the foreground of Imperial affairs, and it was decided that the only way for Britain to protect her interests was to build a railway to Uganda.

In 1869, the opening of the Suez canal had reduced the sea voyage between Britain and India by 11 000 kilometres (7000 miles) or forty days' sailing. To assure unimpeded passage through the canal by her navy and merchant fleet, Britain sought to gain complete control of it. The importance of the canal overshadowed all political considerations, and so in 1882 Britain occupied Egypt. Egypt would be almost uninhabitable were it not for the river Nile, which begins in Uganda, 6500 kilometres (4000 miles) away from its mouth in the Mediterranean. Uganda was thus suddenly invested with immense political importance; for whoever controlled Uganda controlled the Nile (or so the argument went), and the master of the Nile ruled Egypt, including the Suez canal, the vital link to India. It was never quite clear how control of Uganda could in practice affect Egypt. It was very unlikely that any nation could at that time have dammed up the waters of the Nile. Nevertheless, this was the thinking behind probably the most foolhardy railway adventure in history, the building of the line from Mombasa on the Indian Ocean to Lake Victoria.

Above: A startling shot of a steam train crossing a bridge on the South African coast. Vistas such as this have made South Africa a haven for steam enthusiasts. (*A. Jones, ZEFA*)

Above left: A 59 class Garratt locomotive, the *Mount Mgahinga*, arriving at Nairobi with a freight train from Mombasa in 1977. (*Spectrum*)

Top left: An impressive 60 class Garratt in Kenya. The Garratt is the most popular steam locomotive working in Africa today. (*P. B. Whitehouse/Colourviews*)

Right: The arrival at Suez of the first train on the newly built Cairo to Suez railway, on 4 December 1858. Britain's determination to control the Suez canal, opened 11 years later, motivated all her actions in this part of the world, including the construction of railways. (*The Mansell Collection*)

154

The 'lunatic line'

Uganda was declared a British protectorate, and on 11 December 1895 a young English engineer, George Whitehouse, arrived at the sultry east African port of Mombasa. His job was to perform a virtual miracle, to push a railhead through 950 kilometres (600 miles) of unexplored terrain in four years. Directly behind the ancient port of Mombasa lay a small desert, uncharted and seldom crossed. The railway had to cross this desert and then negotiate 480 kilometres (300 miles) of gradually rising savannah and scrub country that teemed with lions, tsetse flies and malaria. After this came a rugged volcanic highland region bisected by a fifty-mile wide rift valley. Even if Whitehouse could man-handle all the engineering equipment down the almost vertical 600 metre (2000 ft) escarpment, there still remained another 160 kilometres (100 miles) across a sponge-like guagmire. It is little wonder that the project was referred to in one British weekly paper as 'the lunatic line'.

Before Whitehouse could push his rails out across the desert he spent several months just setting up a base in Mombasa. Accommodation was the first priority; the Grand Hotel was full, so the men were billeted with local residents or put up in tented camps. The next problem was water. With more than 2500 labourers and technicians enormous quantities were needed, even without considering the needs of the steam locomotives. As the railhead crept out into the desert, locomotives were required to haul 45000 litres (10000 gallons) of water a day to the work gang. The island port of Mombasa was served by small wells that barely supplied the inhabitants, and the railway works caused a man-made drought.

Another problem was the sheer quantity of supplies that had to pass through the port across a narrow wooden bridge to the mainland, a distance of 0.4 kilometres (0.25 miles) and on to the railhead. To cover the 950 kilometre (600 mile) line over 200000 individual 30ft (9.1 metre) rail lengths each weighing 225 kilogrammes (500 lbs) were needed, as well as 1.2 million sleepers (most of which were made of steel, the only protection against white ants). Then there was the real 'hardware'. Whitehouse ordered thirty locomotives, each weighing thirty tonnes, plus tenders, brake vans, goods wagons and passenger coaches. To accommodate such traffic a new port had to be established down the coast, known as Kilindi. To all intents and purposes Whitehouse and his men built a town (which today is the mainland part of Mombasa) before laying a single length of track.

While all this was going on the surveyors had gone ahead to plan the route and mark the obstacles. They were ambushed by the Mazuri tribe, who mounted a revolt against the new invaders of their territory. The army in India had to send a battalion to restore order, and the soldiers remained in attendance to guard the work gangs.

The second part of the advance party were the labourers who cleared the way for the diggers, levellers and platelayers. It was this group who had the hardest job of all. In their path were baobab trees, with trunks up to 3 metres (10 ft) in diameter, and thorn trees, linked by an iron grillwork of creepers and a barricade of secondary growth so dense that cutting parties could sometimes hack through only 275 metres (900 ft) a day.

The advance party would continue forward, and in its wake would

follow the platelayers' gang, supplied with materials by a train that travelled back and forth to them all day. When the railhead had advanced about 15 miles, the platelayers' camp would be moved to the front of the line again. In this manner the 'lunatic line' proceeded.

The climate and terrain were implacable enemies. On a sunny day the temperature could rise to 49 C (120 F). Then there was torrential rain to contend with, as in November 1896 when 356 mm (14 in) fell, slowing the progress down to 24 kilometres (15 miles) in four months. The abnormal rains did not cease until the following January, and as the labourers churned up the ground, leaving water-filled ditches and craters, mosquitoes laid their eggs on the water's surface. In addition, a simple scratch could within hours lead to festering jungle sores. By the end of the year over 500 workers lay in leaking hospital tents suffering from malaria, dysentery, tropical ulcers and pneumonia, and by January 1898 over fifty per cent of the work force were ill. Considering there were only five doctors on the crew, it was miraculous that less than 100 men died that year. In India there was an outbreak of bubonic plague, which delayed the replacement of workers. African labour was inadequate; many of the natives had never seen a pick or a shovel, and there was little time to train them.

Once the railway had traversed the scorching desert, conditions eased. The work speeded up, and a camp was set up on the Tsavo river, where the crew remained for a few weeks while a viaduct was built across the ravine in which the river flowed. All around was arid, dusty terrain, but the Tsavo irrigated a miniature tropical garden. Enthusiasm was high, but was soon dampened when lions began to kill

Above: A Ugandan mail train crossing the bridge over the Nile near Ripon falls, where the river leaves Lake Victoria. It was Uganda's importance as the source of the Nile that led to the building of the 'lunatic line'. (*The Mansell Collection*)

157

Above: A class 13 4-8-4T outside the sheds at Nairobi in 1979. The sheds had three lines of dead steam locos when this picture was taken. (*Spectrum*)

Above left: A Kenyan class 2-8-0 engine after an overhaul at the Nairobi sheds. This locomotive, no. 2458, is now lying idle in the Mombasa yard. (*Colour Library International*)

Left: A pre-war photograph of a 4-6-0 locomotive drawing in at Umuahia on the Port Harcourt–Enugu line in southern Nigeria, Railways have played, and continue to play, a major role in the development of Africa. (*The Mansell Collection*)

workers in the night. Workers vanished without trace, screams were heard as a lion dragged off an unwary man into the bush. So called man-eating lions are rare, and seldom attack, but with a succession of plagues and massive rainfall, the wild life stock was depleted, and for the lions the only likely looking food was the railway labourers. The camps were fortified, and so too were the work sites, yet the lions still claimed many victims. Eventually there was a mass strike and all work on the Tsavo bridge stopped. For weeks the most daring of the man-eaters were hunted, and with each dead lion presented in Mombasa work resumed, until the screams of the next victim testified to another death. The workers would then desert the railhead again.

After many months of lion hunting, the work gang was finally induced to return in full. The railhead was now across the bridge and moving steadily onwards to the great rift valley, having passed Nairobi, where Whitehouse set up new operational headquarters. The year 1899 saw the beginning of a scheduled service between Mombasa and Nairobi.

To reach the rift valley, the railhead covered a 43 kilometre (27 mile)

long incline of 600 metres (2000 ft). The escarpment dropped almost vertically for 450 metres (1500 ft). To lower machines and men to the rift floor was the hardest job of all. This was done by means of cable lifts. The railway had to be taken down the escarpment for a distance of 17 kilometres (10 miles) on eight long viaducts with gentle gradients. After the first attempt at building embankments and other structures a two year drought ended without warning in the middle of the normally dry season, and 120 kilometres (75 miles) of new construction began sinking in a river of mud. Nairobi and Mombasa were separated for over a month.

For twelve months the railhead remained stationary. Then in the late spring of 1900 the work was completed, with one single fatality. The railhead was rushed across the valley floor, and by the autumn the heavy engineering gangs were beginning to take the line up the western escarpment. This was a much easier job, and by New Year's Day 1901 13 kilometres (8 miles) of track skirted and snaked their way to the top. Although the escarpment was just below the equator, being 2750 metres (9000 ft) above sea level meant working in sub-arctic conditions. Snow and sleet battered the camp at the top of the escarpment every day.

Left: South Africa began producing its own steam locomotives commercially in 1966. This extraordinary-looking engine, the first of eight narrow gauge Garratts, was the first result. (*South African Press Services*)

The railway had come 800 kilometres (500 miles), with only 150 kilometres (100 miles), all of them downhill, to go before reaching the lake. However, the local tribe in the area, the Nandi, resented the railway's intrusion, as well as the Indian workers who continually seduced the Nandi boys and girls. The tribesmen started attacking the work gangs and destroying rails and equipment. The soldiers were sent for, and with an armed guard the railhead inched forward.

Throughout the whole project there was constant pressure upon Whitehouse to finish the line. If a tunnel had to be built, he would run a loop round the obstacle while the blasting was going on in order to keep the momentum going. The railhead's progress accelerated to the point where even the telegraph company (an entirely separate venture) failed to keep up. By November 1901 the railhead had advanced to Kibos, a straw-hut village 10 kilometres (6 miles) from the lake. Then disaster struck again. Dysentery swept the camp, and half the crew were laid low. This epidemic was quickly followed by malaria. Then the rains came, turning everything to mud once again. So bad was it that trains could only be unloaded while they were still moving. Once a locomotive stopped the rails would sink and it would gently topple over.

Above: A 4-8-2 locomotive shunting coaches in the yards at Johannesburg in 1975. (*Spectrum*)

The Nandi tribesmen, seeing the situation, began to carry away rails, cables, food, in fact anything that took their fancy, while the weak and feverish railway workers could only watch, unable to do anything. But a month later work commenced yet again, and the rush was on. Five days before Christmas, at 4 o'clock in the afternoon, the line reached Lake Victoria at Port Florence, so called by Whitehouse after Florence Preston, his chief engineer's wife. As Preston and a few railway officials looked on, his wife drove home the last key in the last rail of Britain's newest Imperial steam railway.

Whitehouse was knighted, and the work crew were highly praised in Britain. In 1902 the Union Jack flew above 9.6 million sq kilometres (3.7 million sq miles) of Africa, and the British Empire was at its zenith. In the history of that Empire few adventures can have matched the construction of what Elspeth Huxley the historian has described as 'the most courageous railway in the world'.

This has been a brief account of just one of the many railway lines that helped colonize the dark continent. As each colony has gained independence its railways have developed in various ways. Most have converted to diesel powered locomotives, yet there are many steam engines

still working in Africa, notably in South Africa, where there are rich coal deposits. These steam locomotives have been put to work hauling freight, and shunting goods wagons in the yards.

The most common steam engines to be seen in South Africa, Zimbabwe, Kenya and west Africa are the Beyer-Garratt articulated locomotives, both wood burning and coal-fired. These locomotives weigh 268 tonnes, and have a 4-8-4 + 4-8-4 wheel arrangement. The two sets of driving wheels are set at opposite ends of the locomotive: one set is under the water tank, and the other situated below the fuel tank, with the boiler suspended between them. Most African railways are of a narrow gauge, and their track was originally lightly laid. By using this design of locomotive it was possible to employ heavy, powerful locomotives that, because their weight was distributed equally throughout their length, would not bend and tear the track. As they are articulated they can also negotiate the tight bends so common on the African lines.

The sun may at last have set on the British Empire, but it has not done so on the steam locomotives the Empire brought with it. Not yet at any rate; although, sad to say, at the time of writing, five huge Beyer-Garratts sit rotting on the sidings at Mombasa station, where only 85 years ago George Whitehouse began building his 'lunatic line'.

Above: A Garratt locomotive hauling a passenger train up an incline in eastern South Africa. The length of the train gives an indication of the Garratt's power and ability to haul cars round tight bends. (*J. M. Mehltretter, ZEFA*)

The wide open plains: Russia and China

Russia

'When Emperor Nicholas was asked to decide upon the route of the line between St Petersburg and Moscow, he contemptuously tossed aside the plans, and ordered a map to be unrolled on the table. He put his sword across the map and, indicating a straight line from one city to the other, regardless alike of the rights of way or property, flung his plan at the surveyor saying: "There's your railway."'

John Pendleton, *Our Railways*, 1894

It would be difficult to think of anywhere more in need of railways than the vast expanses of Russia. In the nineteenth century, belated attempts were being made to introduce industrialization to a basically peasant economy. (It is worth remembering that serfdom was not abolished in Russia until 1861.) But, attractive though the idea of railways was in theory, in practice the Tsarist treasury could not contemplate the expense of construction over the huge distances required, local capitalists were less than enthusiastic about railways anyway, and foreign investors were put off by Tsarist bureaucracy.

Railways were built, however, the first of them between the popular resort of Tsarskoye Selo and St Petersburg, the capital. This first section, completed in 1836, was driven by horses, but as the line extended to Pavlovsk, locomotives from the Stephenson locomotive works in Britain were introduced. The gauge was 6 ft (1.83 metres), but was later changed to 5 ft (1.52 metres) when a line was built between Moscow and St Petersburg in 1851. The 5 ft gauge has become the Russian standard. In the following years an increasing number of lines were built by both private and state capital, so that by 1883 there were 23 650 kilometres (14 700 miles) of railways in use.

In the 1880s work began on the massive task of linking European Russia with her Asiatic territories and the eastern shores of the Pacific. By 1890 the lines had reached Chelyabinsk, 1600 kilometres (1000 miles) east of Moscow, but still 7416 kilometres (4608 miles) from Vladivostok on the east coast. The work on the remainder began from both ends at once.

One of the greatest obstacles was Lake Baikal, the world's largest freshwater lake. At first the trains were transported across the lake by ferry, a time-consuming exercise. The first ferry operated at the end of 1901. In 1904, as an experiment, rails were laid across the frozen surface. Unfortunately, this led to disaster when the ice gave way and one of the first trains across was lost. This provoked a final burst of activity to complete the line around the lake, skirting it to the south. Its completion by the end of 1904 provided the final link in a system which permitted uninterrupted rail travel from Moscow to Vladivostok, a distance of 9336 kilometres (5801 miles).

In the east use was initially made of the Chinese Eastern Railway to avoid a large detour round the Chinese frontier. The Russians, however, were anxious to avoid the political and strategic disadvantages of this arrangement, and with the completion of the Amur line in 1916 the Trans-Siberian Railway at last ran wholly on Russian soil. A year later came the Revolution, and the entire Russian network of 75 500 kilometres (43 900 miles) was nationalized.

The 5 ft (1.52 metre) gauge which became the standard for Russian railways permitted the development of huge locomotives. The rolling stock could be 11 ft 6 in (3.5 metres) wide, and as high as 17 ft (5.2 metres). Although foreign, especially American, influence was very important in Russian railway development, a domestic steam locomotive industry was quick to organize. In 1882 Alexander Borodin built the world's first stationary test laboratory for locomotives.

One constant preoccupation of the Russian railway planners was the striving for standardization, leading to the employment of large numbers of a few selected engine types. For example, the 'E' class 0-10-0 freight locomotive, which was first introduced in 1912, eventually numbered 14 000 engines. This was the engine chosen by the new Soviet government as the basis for railway reconstruction after the ravages of World War I and the Russian Civil War. In 1922 a single order was made for 1000 engines from the Swedish NOHAB locomotive company. This was the largest single order made by any railway in the world. The largest Russian class, the 0-8-0 freight engine, numbered 8000, built between 1891 and 1923.

The inter-war years were characterized by acute shortages of finance, leading to weaknesses in the construction of the railways. Soviet railway development was hampered by the introduction of extremely large, unwieldy locomotives, and by Stalinism. In 1932 the USSR bought the largest Garratt articulated locomotive ever built, a 4-8-2 + 2-8-4 R-01

Above: Construction work on the Trans-Siberian Railway near Khabarovka, eastern Siberia; from *Harper's New Monthly Magazine*, June 1898. Conditions for the railway workers were extremely hard, and convict labour was widely used. (*Peter Newark's Historical Pictures*)

165

which weighed 267 tonnes and had a tractive effort of 35 700 kilogrammes (78 700 lbs). A year later the 2-8-4 Stalin class was introduced. This massive engine was designed to haul 800 tonnes at 40 km/h (25 mph) uphill. The search for even bigger locomotives led to the 4-14-4 engine built in 1934. This proved too rigid for operations on Soviet lines, and like so many things in the Stalin era, just 'disappeared'.

During World War II, railways in Russia proved vital to the country's survival in her fight against the invading German forces, providing front line troops with essential supplies from factories and depots that had been relocated in the east. After the war, and especially after the death of Stalin, railway modernization began on a huge scale. The last Soviet steam engines were the 2-10-0 'L' class, of which 4700 were built, the 2-10-2 and the 4-8-4 class P36, all built in 1956. It was in that same year that the steam engine lost its place in future railway plans in Russia. A few steam engines still exist on small local lines and industrial sites, but they have now permanently disappeared from the main lines.

Chinese railways: inscrutable indecision

Chinese society at the beginning of the railway age was characterized by a deeply ingrained suspicion of all outsiders. This vast Empire had hidden behind its Great Wall since before the days of Marco Polo. During the latter half of the nineteenth century this state of affairs was being disturbed by the firm determination of foreigners to exploit China's resources and markets, by fair means or otherwise. The Chinese attitude towards railways as obvious symbols of foreign influence naturally reflected this situation.

The first line in the Empire was built in 1876, running the 20 miles

Above: The *Celestial Empire* leaves Shanghai in 1876 to run the 32 kilometres (20 miles) to Woosung. A year later this whole railway was dismantled and moved to Taiwan (Formosa). (*Mary Evans Picture Library*)

(32 kilometres) from Shanghai to Woosung. British commercial interests obtained permission for a road on this route. Instead they built a railway with a 2 ft 6 in (0.76 metre) gauge, running two 0-4-0 saddle tank engines on it. In the following year local suspicion came to a head when a local man was killed by a train. There were riots and demonstrations, often very violent, against the railway, which prompted the government to buy up the line, dismantle it and ship it to Formosa (now Taiwan).

Another line, again British, ran the 160 kilometres (100 miles) from Peking to the Kaiping coalfields, but until 1891 it was mule driven. In that year a British engineer at one of the mines built an engine from scrap iron and put it into service much to the chagrin of the Chinese. This engine was called the *Rocket of China*. The operating gauge of the line was British standard, a fact which became important as this Kaiping tramway was extended to become the Peking to Mukden main line, which eventually linked into the Trans-Siberian Railway *en route* to Moscow.

A great fear among local rulers in China was that the railway's through routes would rob them of customs duties. The only way round these impediments was an Imperial decree. At this time Emperor Kuang Hsu was still a child, so effective power lay in the hands of his mother, the Empress. It is said the forward-looking statesman Li Hung-Chang finally won both of them over to the cause of railway development by

Above: Peking station in 1976. China may have the largest number of working steam trains in the world. (*P. B. Whitehouse/ Colourviews*)

presenting the child Emperor with a clockwork train set. But China was already lagging seriously behind other parts of the world, and still had only 200 kilometres (125 miles) of track by 1890.

The Sino-Japanese war of 1895 and the Russo-Japanese war of 1904–5 had strong effects on the development of Chinese railways: the first by weakening China, and drawing the attention of interested parties to the strategic value of railways across Chinese territory, the second by transferring part of the newly built Russian lines of Manchuria to Japanese control. By 1905 the Manchurian railways connecting China to the Trans-Siberian route were split between the Japanese 3 ft 6 in (1.07 metre) gauge and the Russian 5 ft (1.52 metre) width. This part of the country was not destined to rest under the control of any one country for long: it fell into Japanese hands in the 1930s, was taken over by the Russians in 1945, and was finally returned to China in 1952.

Not until 1909 was a railway line built by Chinese skill and money alone. This was the Peking–Kalgan line, 210 kilometres (130 miles) long. Meanwhile more lines were being built by the Chinese with foreign capital, and these were collected under the umbrella title of the Chinese Government Railways. But the widespread resentment of foreign involvement persisted, and the central government's apparent readiness to consort with outsiders fuelled the flames of discord already burning between it and the provinces. The railways became an important focus for the unrest which led to the collapse of the Manchu

Right: A rare view indeed! Steam locomotives in a shunting yard at Tangshan, China. (*P. B. Whitehouse/Colourviews*)

dynasty and the foundation of the Chinese Republic. The new government gradually proceeded on a course towards nationalization. Attempts were made to expand the Chinese rail system, but the invasions and civil wars of the 1930s and '40s gave this little chance of success.

A more settled climate, following the Maoist assumption of power in 1949, enabled the newly renamed Chinese Peoples' Railways to sort out many of their problems. Much of the development work through the 1950s was aided by Russia, leading to a strong Russian influence in operating style. This influence continued long after the cooling of relations between Moscow and Peking.

Today, despite inroads made by electrification and diesel locomotion, steam still accounts for a majority of Chinese railway movement. The veil of secrecy is beginning to lift over the Chinese mainland. The story remains to be told of what British and Russian locomotives are still in use. The first train spotters allowed into China will have a priceless experience, as China may well have the largest corps of steam locomotives active in the world today.

Left: Since the rebuilding there of the Shanghai-Woosung railway trains have come a long way on Taiwan. Here a Chinese 4-6-0 locomotive waits at Taichung station. (*S. Sammer, ZEFA*)

171

The longest straight line in the world

When the first steam train ran in Australia in 1854, the country was only 63 years old. The line on which it ran connected Melbourne with its port, Sandridge, 4 kilometres (2.5 miles) away, and the track was laid in a broad gauge of 1.6 metres (5 ft 3 in). When the Sydney to Parramatta line, the first railway in New South Wales, opened in 1855 with the British standard gauge of 1.43 metres (4 ft 8½ in) a new 'gauge war' had been started, which, unlike the original disagreement between Brunel and Stephenson in Britain, lasted for 110 years and became the predominant feature of Australian railways.

The Sydney line soon began to lose money, but was rescued by the New South Wales government, making it the first railway in the British Empire to be nationalized. The rail system began to radiate outwards from the important coastal cities in order that the central and northern areas could be explored and exploited. Progress was slow because of the arduous conditions and acute lack of finance, which required the various provincial governments to initiate construction.

As more lines were opened the gauge war became more and more entangled. The British government strongly advised the Australian authorities to standardize their gauges, before it became too costly to change. Accordingly, South Australia passed an Act specifying that all its railways were to be of British standard gauge. However, in New South Wales the chief railway engineer, Francis Shields, was an Irishman, as were most of the population, and he persuaded the NSW government to adopt the 'Irish gauge' of 1.6 metres (5 ft 3 in). Six months later Victoria adopted the Irish width also. Later, under the guidance of Shields' successor, a Scot, New South Wales reversed its decision and decided that all new railways would be of British standard gauge. Victoria, with a partially built railway system standardized in the Irish gauge to fall in with what had previously been supposed to be New South Wales' intentions, objected vigorously, and was supported by South Australia, which had by now also ordered rolling stock in the broad gauge. Both colonies declared that it would be too expensive to change gauges yet again, and a gauge war became inevitable.

Nothing could stop the ever-increasing spread of rail links through the length and breadth of Australia, with each colony maintaining its chosen gauge. By 1945 there were five gauge widths in use. From the 1860s until 1970 parliamentary committees, railway engineers, newspapers, and disgruntled passengers and freight customers bemoaned the situation, argued the case, and proposed the most outlandish solutions to the break-of-gauge problem.

In 1930 the first major construction of a standardized inter-colonial railway took place with the building of a 1.43 metre (4 ft 8½ in) gauge line from Brisbane to Grafton in Queensland, which abolished the

Above right: An American-built 4-8-2 Mountain class locomotive, exported to Australia where it first appeared in 1911. Ideally suited to the fast passenger routes, it was equipped with a feedwater heater to enable it to cross the vast waterless deserts of Australia. (*Australian Information Bureau*)

Right: A train on one of Australia's stock routes, taking cattle to South Australia from the loading yards at Alice Springs. Steam engines have now disappeared from Australian lines. (*Australian Information Bureau*)

Above: An early Australian 4-4-0, no. 176, now on display at the New South Wales Rail Transport Museum, Thirlmere. (*Spectrum*)

break in gauge between Sydney and Brisbane. During the work on the line however the full immensity of the task of standardizing the gauges became clear. Bridges, tunnels, stations, culverts and cuttings all needed adjustment. The cost of the operation was enormous. When in 1957 the Victorian Minister of Transport announced the unification of the Melbourne–Sydney line, it was estimated that it would cost around £200 000 000 – a fantastic sum, but when weighed against the savings on operational costs it was deemed necessary if Australia's railways were to survive as profit-making concerns.

The increasing competition from road transport greatly accelerated the changeover work. Ministers and others stressed that the break-in-gauge system had nearly become a national tragedy in World War II by preventing east coast steel mills from obtaining sufficient ore from the mines in southern and western states. The situation had forced the concentration of munitions stockpiles at break points, creating easy targets for enemy air raids. Furthermore, three army divisions had had to be moved from Western Australia to face a threatened Japanese invasion of the east coast. To move the divisions to meet this threat only one train a day was possible for the 3500 kilometre (2200 mile) transfer, with four breaks of gauge causing lengthy holdups. Had there

been a uniform gauge throughout, 24 trains each way per day could have been run.

Even now, the effects of the gauge war (which, unlike in Britain, was never a cause of real bitterness, but which for so long presented everybody with infuriating problems) are still reflected in Australia in the high travel and freight fares. The whole Australian railway system has had to be rationalized, a process which continues to date, with the completion scheduled for 1980 of the Adelaide to Port Pirie line in South Australia, where ironically the trouble started. All the main cities are now connected by a standard gauge rail link.

The most important challenge facing Australia's railways was apparent from the earliest days: to link Perth on the west coast with Adelaide, Melbourne and Sydney in the south and east. This meant pushing a track out across the Nullarbor Plain in Western Australia, on which there were virtually no trees, water, animals or people, just a vast expanse of dust and scorching heat. The onset of the First World War made the project a matter of strategic importance, and it was further encouraged by the discovery of gold at Kalgoorlie and in the surrounding area. When it was built, in 1917, the line followed a 1690 kilometre (1051 mile) route across barren desert: and for 478 kilometres

Above: An Australian-built 4-6-2 Pacific of the NSW Railway on shunting duty at the Alexandria yards, Sydney. (*Colour Library International*)

175

Right: An aerial view of
part of 'the longest straight
line in the world', the
railway line stretching
nearly 480 kilometres (300
miles) straight across the
Nullarbor plain, a flat sandy
desert 260 000 sq kilometres
(100 000 sq miles) in area.
(*Australian Information
Bureau*)

(297 miles) the track continues in a dead straight line, the longest straight line in the world.

Because of the arid conditions, during the building of the line camels were used for carrying supplies. It was so bad at some points that the continually billowing sand would cover the rails as quickly as they were laid. The construction crew lived on salt beef, bread and rice, digging in each night as the railhead moved forward.

By day the work gangs toiled in temperatures of 49°C (120°F), while by night they shivered in temperatures that were sub-zero in winter. The biggest problem however was not the heat but the water supply. The crew had to sink bore holes to supply themselves, but this impure water soon corroded the boiler tubes of the locomotives being used on the construction.

Locomotives were ordered from Britain – 4-6-0s for passenger trains, 2-8-0s for freight, built by the Northern British Locomotive Works in Glasgow. The strategic importance of the line ensured prompt delivery, despite the heavy demands on British locomotive works for engines to supply to the Allied forces in France and Belgium. The first eastbound train finally steamed out of Kalgoorlie on 25 October 1917.

Along this line now runs the famous Trans-Australian Indian Pacific express. The first locomotives to pull this transcontinental luxury train were Baldwin type class 36 4-6-0s, but these were soon replaced by 4-6-2s built by the Australian Clyde Locomotive Works. The same shops produced 4-8-2 freight engines that were in use up to and during the Second World War. After the war, however, the steam locomotives were edged out of the transcontinental route by diesels, which did not

require vast amounts of water. In the early days of the route, when it was operated by steam engines, every fifth train had to bring fuel and water out for the other locomotives, to be left for them along the line.

Australia contributed very little in the way of steam locomotive design, her railway companies tending to place orders in Britain, very often for American-style engines. At the beginning of this century an English engineer, Herbert Garratt, was working for the New South Wales Government Railway, and saw the damage that heavy locomotives could inflict on light track such as composed much of the Australian system. There was no easy answer to this, as small locomotives could do no more than supply localized traffic, while for the long-distance freight runs much bigger machines, liable to tear up the track, were needed. On returning to England in 1906, he designed the famous Garratt articulated locomotive as a solution to the problem – although most of the essential work was in fact done by his chief engineer, Sam Jackson. The first Garratts were delivered to Tasmanian Railways in 1909. Their advantage was that, though awesome engines, they ran happily on light rails. Within a few years they could be seen on the narrow gauge lines of Australia, Africa and South America. Garratt, however, died too early to witness the success of his innovation.

Steam engines have not been a part of the Australian railway scene since the early 1960s. Many of the steam locomotives that were ousted by the diesels and electrics were sold to poorer lines in Indonesia, Malaysia and Singapore. Most of those that could not be sold made one final journey, to the breaker's yard.

Steam today and tomorrow

In this book we have taken a look at just some of the many and varied stories of the spread of steam railways round the world. The one feature common to most of these stories is their ending: the phasing out of the steam locomotive in favour of diesel and electric engines. The sad fact is that steam is less efficient than modern forms of traction. Oil is much easier to handle than coal, and coal is used more efficiently when burned at a central power station, rather than in thousands of small locomotive boilers.

Steam locomotives are far from dead, though. In some countries, notably South Africa and India, they still work the main lines. South Africa has coal to spare for use in her 1911 locomotives, while India, not sharing the modern obsession with speed, will be relying on her 2597 steam engines for many years to come. Many other countries supplement their locomotive power with steam, and industrial and mining complexes often make use of ageing tank engines rather than buy new stock.

Those in western countries wishing to see steam locomotives in all their glory and excitement must turn to the preservation societies. As steam was phased out in Britain, Europe, the United States and Australia, thousands of societies sprang up to preserve locomotives, rolling stock and railway buildings before they were destroyed for ever.

In Britain there are over 100 steam-powered privately owned railways. Some are just museums, with a short length of track on which a couple of engines can shunt to and fro; but others, like the Bluebell Railway in Sussex, are full railway systems. The Bluebell was salvaged from the line that connected Horsted Keynes with East Grinstead, and opened in 1959, four years after British Railways closed the service. Within a decade the line was carrying 250 000 passengers a year.

Throughout the summer, and some of the winter, the Bluebell runs a timetable service on the 8 kilometres (5 miles) between Sheffield Park station and Horsted Keynes. Locals use the line as a regular form of transport, but the majority of passengers are visitors who just want the pleasure of travelling on a steam train. The Bluebell Railway Society plans to rebuild the missing section of track running between Horsted Keynes and East Grinstead, a distance of 10 kilometres (6 miles). This section was closed under the Beeching plan, and much of the land was sold. The difficult task remains for the society of negotiating with local landowners to make a path available for the proposed extension, not an easy matter for a charitable organization. Gone are the days of 'cut-and-thrust' railway progress.

Millions of pounds in voluntary donations have been spent on restoring steam locomotives, many of which had already been dismantled. Ex-steam engineers and self-taught mechanics have put years into piecing

Right: The *Duke of Edinburgh,* a restored Pacific, pulling a train of enthusiasts through the Pichi Richi Pass, 290 kilometres (180 miles) north of Adelaide, South Australia, on a line which has been preserved by public donations for the running of steam trains. (*Australian Information Bureau*)

together the steam giants of the past, so that in the present they can be enjoyed and appreciated by those who missed the age of steam railways.

What future for steam?

For all practical purposes, the steam railway in the industrialized northern hemisphere is a thing of the past. However, some talk is now heard about possible new applications of steam in locomotives. British Rail research engineers have been looking at steam turbines and, although they see no immediate future for them on the railways, these engines may well appear one day. 'Turbomotives' were employed on British Railways in the late 1950s, but their potential was lost in the forward march to diesels. The London, Midland and Scottish had two 4-6-0s of this type, built by English Electric. Some research has been carried out in the United States into nuclear-powered steam turbines, but as yet there is no definite news of concrete proposals. Meanwhile, the Argentinian State Railways are conducting studies on what they

describe as 'new ways of developing steam power for railway use'. In Japan, the National Railway has been forced to consider running steam services from Takashima to Yamashita, after receiving a petition from 30 Japanese city authorities who felt that the potential of steam loco-motion had not been exhausted.

Back in Britain, a section of suburban line operated by London Transport may allow the local railway committee to run a weekend steam service between Epping and Ongar. At present the line is losing hundreds of thousands of pounds each year, and the revenue gained from the attraction that steam trains would have could tip the balance and stave off closure of the line. The Epping to Ongar line is part of the overground section of the London Underground Central Line, which is entirely electric.

Perhaps the most exciting event in recent steam affairs is the re-run of the Rainhill trials and the 150th anniversary of the opening of the Liverpool and Manchester Railway. All three engines that took part in 1829 have been reproduced as part of a 3-year-long project. The first

Right: A moment's reflection while waiting at signals for the driver and stoker of a locomotive at the Crown Mines, South Africa. (*Interfoto Archives*)

engine completed was the *Rocket*, built in Gateshead, England, which was run on a 90 metre (300 ft) stretch of rail in Hyde Park in the autumn of 1979. *Novelty* is still under construction at the time of writing, while the *Sans Pareil*, although built, is still undergoing modifications and tests.

In the late spring of 1980, the three engines will compete, as in the original trials, and under the same strict conditions. Indeed, the construction of these replicas has embodied the same air of competition. Each engine has been constructed by a separate locomotive works specially opened for the project. The *Rocket* was built under the guidance of engineer Mike Satows, with a work force consisting of young apprentices who were learning their chosen trades during the project. Wherever possible the same basic techniques were employed as were used by Stephenson 150 years ago. This did present problems. For

example, the wheelwright had trouble using wood that was unseasoned; and the boiler had to meet high safety standards set down by the government, a consideration that never arose during the original trials.

The re-run of the Rainhill trials is an exciting prospect, and British Rail will be arranging for special steam trains to run from Liverpool and Manchester to ferry the thousands of visitors that have already booked seats at the enclosure in Rainhill. You will remember that Timothy Hackworth never really recovered his pride after losing the original trials. On the day of the re-run, his great granddaughter will be on the footplate of the *Sans Pareil*. Hackworth always suspected that Stephenson, who had helped him with the casting of the cylinders for the *Sans Pareil*, had sabotaged his engine. We shall never know whether there was any truth in that, but what an odd irony it would be if, after 150 years, Timothy Hackworth finally beat the *Rocket* and won the Rainhill trials.

Above: This is very nearly where we began. The *Rocket* Mark II, built for the re-run of the Rainhill trials in May 1980, pulls into St Pancras station, London, in March 1980 on a run celebrating the 150th anniversary of the first mail to be carried by train. (The Guardian)

Right: The old and the new at Paddington station, London. The *King George V,* first of the King class locomotives that once worked the Great Western Railway, pulls out with an enthusiasts' special past its counterpart of today, the Inter-City 125 High Speed Train. (*John Titlow*)

How a steam locomotive works

The *Caerphilly Castle*, a superheated 4-6-0 four-cylinder Castle class express locomotive, built in 1923 for the Great Western Railway in England. It is now on permanent display at the Science Museum, London.

When introduced, the *Caerphilly Castle* was the most powerful passenger express locomotive in Britain. Nevertheless its mechanical workings, shown here in this sectional diagram, are based upon the same principles which governed the building of steam locomotives from the earliest examples right up to the very last to be produced.

Cold air passes through the ventilator into a firebox, where it is heated by a fire kept up by coal passed, either automatically or by hand shovel, through the firedoor. The resultant hot gasses and smoke then flow round the brick arch and along the heater tubes. These tubes are immersed in water, and when the passage of the hot gasses causes their surface to heat up, they heat the

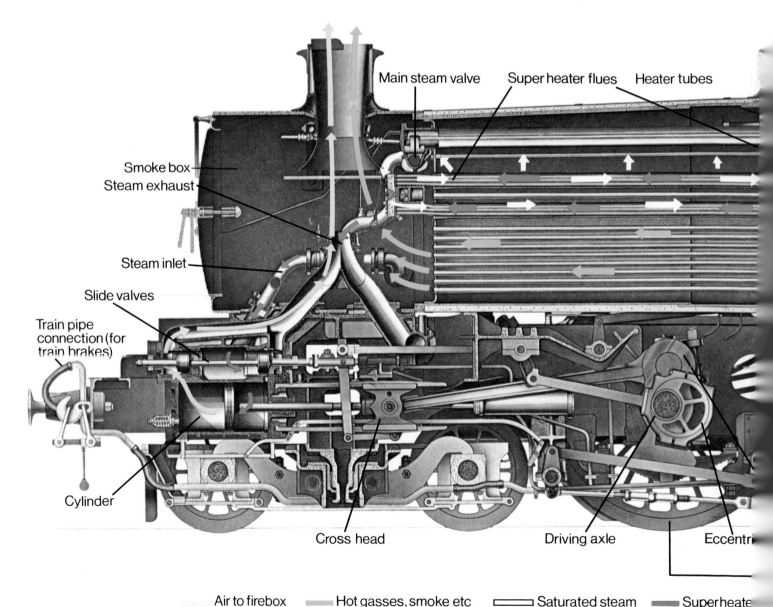

Main steam valve   Super heater flues   Heater tubes

Smoke box
Steam exhaust
Steam inlet
Slide valves
Train pipe connection (for train brakes)
Cylinder
Cross head
Driving axle
Eccentri

Air to firebox   Hot gasses, smoke etc   Saturated steam   Superheate surrounding water and produce steam. The steam rises towards the top of the boiler, and pressure builds up on the steam valves. Two safety valves, in the steam dome in this locomotive, check that the pressure does not become excessive. The main steam valve is operated by the regulator handle in the driver's cab. The saturated or 'wet' steam passes through this and, in a superheated locomotive such as the *Caerphilly Castle*, enters the superheater flues. Meanwhile a pipe also feeds steam from the boiler to the 'steam stand' or 'fountain'. This supplies steam for powering auxiliaries, such as the train's brakes and the water feed from the tender. It also supplies the whistle.

The superheater flues contain tightly packed 'elements', or small pipes, constructed in such a way that the saturated or 'wet' steam is forced to pass up and down the flue four times before emerging. This superheated, more efficient steam is then directed down pipes to the cylinders. The entry of steam into the cylinders is regulated by slide valves, moved back and forth by the movement of the Walschaert valve gear system which translates the motion of the piston rod into the rotation of the wheels. The steam thus enters the cylinder from alternate sides; the alternate pressure produces continuous movement of the piston and, thus, of the wheels.

When the slide valve opens again to allow the exhausted steam out of the cylinder, it is conveyed by an exhaust pipe up to the smoke box, where it mingles with the hot gasses and smoke from the heater tubes, and then up through the chimney into the atmosphere.

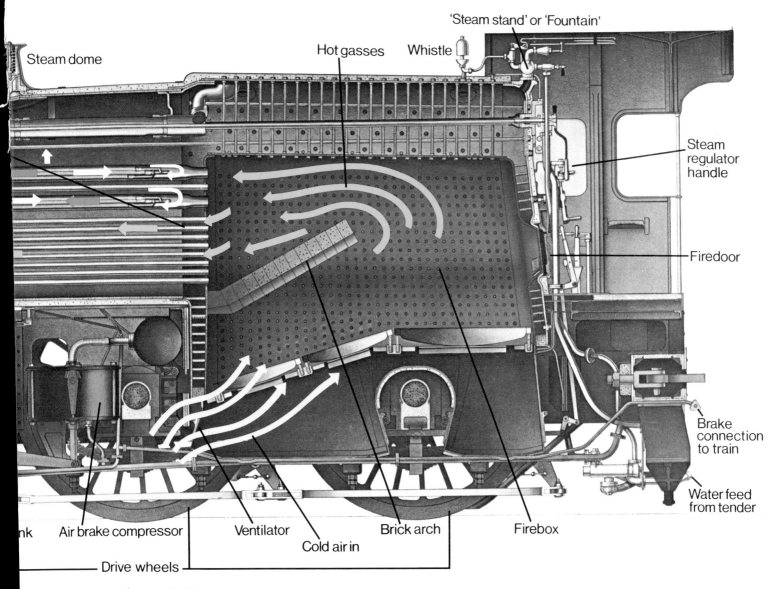

'Steam stand' or 'Fountain'

Hot gasses

Whistle

Steam dome

Steam regulator handle

Firedoor

Brake connection to train

Water feed from tender

nk   Air brake compressor

Ventilator

Cold air in

Brick arch

Firebox

Drive wheels

Exhaust (expanded) steam

Index

Page numbers in roman type denote textual references; those in italics denote relevant illustrations.